MASTERS *AND* SERVANTS *IN* TUDOR ENGLAND

ALISON SIM

SUTTON PUBLISHING

First published in 2006 by
Sutton Publishing Limited . Phoenix Mill
Thrupp . Stroud . Gloucestershire . GL5 2BU

British Library Cataloguing in Publication Data
A catalogue record for this book is available from the British Library.

ISBN 0-7509-4017-4

Front and rear endpapers: A black trumpeter on the Westminster Tournament Roll.
(By permission of The College of Arms, London)

To Allan, with love

Typeset in 11/14.5pt Sabon.
Typesetting and origination by
Sutton Publishing Limited.
Printed and bound in England by
J.H. Haynes & Co. Ltd, Sparkford.

Contents

List of Plates

BLACK AND WHITE

List of Plates

COLOUR

Introduction

The very word 'servant' conjures up visions of a private world tucked away behind a discreet green baize door. To modern minds, servants in the past were expected to know their place and never presume to get too familiar with their employers. The concept that your personal servant might also be a close friend whose social life you shared seems odd to us, but was quite normal to the Tudors.

The idea that working as a servant was in itself somehow demeaning simply didn't exist. Of course you were expected to show respect to your employer, but the simple fact that you were a servant didn't make you inferior. Sixteenth-century houses were not designed with carefully separated accommodation for servants and masters. Lower down the social scale, where there often wasn't a great deal of space in most houses, servants could even share accommodation with members of the family. Even at the top level, personal servants always had to be within calling distance of their master or mistress, and so slept close to them. Masters and servants were not strictly segregated.

For many young people being a servant was simply a recognised part of growing up. For many it was a way of learning the skills involved in running a house and a farm while also earning money at the same time. For children born higher up the social scale, working as a personal attendant to a great person in a large household provided a variety of opportunities. For one thing, you would get to know important people who might help your career in the future. You would gain social polish and also practical skills that could lead to the very highest offices if you were talented and lucky. It was because personal service in a great household could lead to better things that working as a servant was not looked down on. Indeed, the role of servants was so closely tied in with the great households that you need some idea of what they were and how they worked in order to understand how the status of servants changed. As the households declined, so too did the whole status of servants.

A great household could consist of incredibly large numbers of people. In Henry VIII's reign the Earl of Northumberland employed 166 people in his household. The Earl of Derby employed 118 servants in 1587 and William Cecil as Baron Burghley around 120. While many of these servants performed practical work such as cleaning and cooking, others were gentlemen servants who were employed in administration, or even in roles that were more a matter of prestige than of usefulness.

There were several reasons why lords kept so many servants, not all of them connected with mere vanity. One reason was the idea of lordly magnificence. The theory was that great people were expected to have a lifestyle that reflected their status. They had to wear the right sort of clothes, eat lavish foods and entertain the right people in a suitably grand way. Most of all, they were expected to employ large numbers of people as an expression of their wealth and power. Naturally, such living was not cheap, and families could be – and were – ruined by the expense if careful management was lacking. Indeed, the expense of the large household was one of the reasons why it went out of fashion. Even so, while the system lasted, personal service could bring considerable profit.

Part of the idea of magnificence involved raising a great many of the ordinary routines of life surrounding a lord to heights of ceremony. Several books were produced in the late fifteenth and sixteenth centuries explaining the intricate details of how lords and ladies were to be woken, bathed, dressed, fed and put to bed. Meals, especially dinner, the main meal of the day, were served with a ceremoniousness that seems almost incredible today. In a very hierarchical society, it was also considered fitting that those whose duties brought them into close personal contact with the lord should themselves be at least of the rank of gentleman. This is why there was so much work for gentlemen in noble houses.

On the other hand, the work that the lord had to offer those of higher status was not all ceremonial. Lords owned large estates that needed to be managed, and managed well if the family was to thrive. Likewise, great men often held high office in government. Chief government officials have always needed a great deal of administrative support, but in Tudor times crown officials were expected to both put together and pay for their own team. This meant that great households included men who were doing very important administrative work for their employer, but who might also have a ceremonial job that involved such duties as helping to serve dinner, especially on the greatest occasions, such as royal visits.

A young boy entering a great household would be taught all the ceremonial duties necessary for attending a lord but would also be given a good general education. If he did well, he could progress in the service of his lord and perhaps even achieve a place at court. Cecil himself worked in the household of Edward Seymour, Duke of Somerset, before he became Principal Secretary of State in 1550. Opportunities for girls, on the other hand, were virtually non-existent. The great households, even those headed by a woman rather than a man, were staffed almost entirely by men. Usually the only females in grand households were the lord's wife, his unmarried daughters and the small number of female attendants who looked after them and acted as their companions. The only female lower-class servant that the household was likely to employ would be the laundress.

Even if you were not particularly gifted and destined for great things, many gentlemen jumped at the chance to work in a great household. It was a particularly good option for younger sons who were not going to inherit the family wealth. For them, it was a chance to enjoy a very pleasant lifestyle without having to make enough money to set themselves up independently. There were, of course, drawbacks. In his famous book *Utopia*, Thomas More complained about the large numbers of 'idle persons' that such men kept, and pointed out that if these 'idle persons' became sick, they often found themselves thrown out of their cosy little job with nowhere to go. Even so, plenty of young gentlemen seem to have been willing to take such work, not least as it added substantially to your prestige to work in the household of a great man. It could also add considerably to your safety, as many of a lord's household formed what was in effect his private army.

People generally assume that in the sixteenth century private armies died out and all military power was safely centred in the hands of the monarch. The Tudors did indeed do all they could to limit private armies, but the greatest nobles could still muster considerable numbers of men even in the late sixteenth century. In 1588, at the time of the Armada crisis, the Earl of Pembroke wrote to Queen Elizabeth offering her three hundred cavalry and five hundred foot-soldiers, all armed from his own personal arsenal. Clearly the nobility were still capable of causing trouble if they wanted to. It says a great deal about Elizabeth's determination to avoid such trouble that she refused the earl's offer, despite the depth of the crisis.[1]

Society was a great deal more violent even in Tudor times than many people realise. The opening scene of *Romeo and Juliet*, where men from the households of the two warring families fight for no real reason, would have been just as recognisable in sixteenth-century London as in Italy. Under the circumstances, it was understandable that gentlemen were happy to enjoy the protection that working for a noble could bring.

Even those who didn't work in a noble household were often pleased to wear a great man's livery, or uniform, which was given to various people as a way of showing that that person had their protection. The receiver of the livery would enjoy not only the prestige of wearing it, but also several practical benefits. People might well think twice about taking someone with a great lord's protection to court, for example. The right to wear such livery was something that people were even prepared to pay for. As late as 1593 Charles Chester told Gelli Myrich, steward to the Earl of Essex, that he would give him £100 if he could obtain the earl's livery for him. The use of such livery was anything but subtle. In the early years of Elizabeth's reign there was a power struggle between the Earl of Leicester and William Cecil. At the time it was alleged that in every shire there were justices of the peace who openly wore Leicester's livery.[2]

The good news from the monarch's point of view was that during the course of the sixteenth century the need for private armies faded. One of the reasons that had helped keep them going had been that, whatever the royal misgivings, the crown did sometimes call on the aristocracy to provide men and arms. As a result the tenants of the aristocracy were still often obliged to give military service, as well as rent, to their landlords. As late as 1599 the Earl of Rutland called his tenants to help on his Irish expedition. However, after James I came to the throne in 1603 the crown stopped making these demands. This changed the whole nature of the relationship between landlords and tenants, and also meant there was no longer any need to employ gentlemen in the household to form the core of a bodyguard. Even great men such as the Dukes of Buckingham and Salisbury felt no need for a large bodyguard in the seventeenth century.[3]

The most important of the great households was, of course, the royal court. In royal circles personal service to the monarch was a great prize. It gave you regular access to the private apartments, where you could hear everything that was going on. Such knowledge could be passed on to members of your family, and could even be sold for hard cash. Even relatively small details could be vital. In Elizabeth I's reign maids of honour and ladies-in-waiting could expect to be paid for a tip-off about the queen's mood, so that petitioners knew when to approach her to ask for favours. They could also try to persuade the queen to grant private audiences to certain individuals, or simply mention someone's name in the royal presence at the right time. In 1587 the Earl of Rutland was told that he was 'much beholden to Mistress Radcliffe (a lady of the privy chamber); she daily doth good offices for you. She is worthy to be presented with something.'[4] The pay normally took the form of a gift rather than money, but sometimes the gifts could be very valuable, like a set of tapestries or a pair of horses. You were also well placed to ask favours for yourself or for a member of your family, as you were constantly in the royal presence. The inconveniences of court life, many though they were, paled into insignificance beside the advantages if you were fortunate.

It could still be worth your while to come to court even if you knew that dirty manual work was the best you could expect. Maids of honour and ladies-in-waiting were never given such work to do, but of course the royal apartments had to be kept clean and warm, just like the other rooms. This work was done instead by the chamberers, but even they were gentlemen's daughters. The potential profits to be gained from working directly in the royal apartments were such that it was well worth doing even the dirty work.

If those at the very top of society were happy to be personal attendants then it is understandable that service was not despised further down society. It is not surprising that there was such a different attitude to servants. When someone in Tudor times referred to their family, they didn't mean just their relatives but also anyone who lived under their roof, including the servants. Even lowly apprentices became part of their master's family because they lived with them, so that the relationship between master and apprentice was much more personal than that between a modern employer and employee.

Another factor that affected the way servants were viewed was rich people's attitude to work. In the sixteenth century even wealthy people were not brought up to a life of elegant idleness. Wealthy women were often responsible for the running of the family estates, not least because the men were away at court. Merchants' wives were often actively involved in running the family business. This meant that wealthy people didn't have to disassociate themselves from their servants simply to make the point that they didn't do practical work themselves.

The whole situation began to change by the end of the century as the great households started to disappear. By the mid-seventeenth century they had gone. The court finally stopped travelling round and became centred on London, so that whether they liked it or not courtiers had to spend a great deal of time in the city. Most of them seem to have liked it very much indeed as the city offered social possibilities that were unimaginable in the country. At the same time coaches also became more common, so that most wealthy families owned one. They lacked springing, but even so they made travel much easier, so that making the journey to London from the country became a great deal simpler. The London season was born, and a fine house in London became a necessity for anyone with ambitions at court.

Great lords both temporal and spiritual had owned London houses for centuries. The king's business of one kind or another often brought the aristocracy to the city, so a place for you and your household to stay was very useful. London had also long been the best place in the country to buy luxury goods of all kinds, so you or senior members of your household might come on shopping expeditions. You could also mix business with pleasure and do a little entertaining while you were there. In 1421 Elizabeth Berkeley, Countess of Warwick, came to London for a month to pursue her case against the crown for possession of the Berkeley lands and to entertain her friends. She stayed at the Berkeley Inn (large houses were often known as inns). However, the inns of the Middle Ages and the Renaissance town houses were very different buildings.

Inns like Elizabeth Berkeley's were essentially designed to be a kind of blank stage. The building itself was not particularly impressive when it was empty. It was only when the owner was in residence that everything changed. Lavish hangings decorated the walls and gold and silver plate was put on display, transforming the building into a palace. The post-Renaissance town house was totally different. An impressive exterior, built in the latest style, was considered necessary to demonstrate not only the owner's wealth but also his excellent taste. The interior was decorated with lavish works of art and fine furniture. Such a house was much more expensive to build and maintain than a medieval inn.[5] For one thing, constant rebuilding and redecorating were required to keep the house up to date.

The changes made a big difference to the appearance of the city. By 1560 about half the peers owned houses in London and a row of palaces linked the Strand to Westminster. By the early seventeenth century these palaces were being broken up into smaller premises as the important men no longer needed huge houses to accommodate their households. Instead, they wanted smaller, more fashionable town houses. Covent Garden, Drury Lane and St Martin's Lane were all built at this time as housing for the aristocracy.

Landed estates continued to be an important source of income, and were also vital for maintaining status. The need for influence in parliament was also growing, and such tenants as did have the right to vote would be expected to do so according to the landlord's wishes. An impressive country residence was also a necessity for a man who wished to be taken seriously, so country houses too had to be built, or rebuilt, in the latest style and suitably furnished. As a result huge sums of money were spent on building. The Duke of Somerset spent £15,000 on Somerset House and Syon House in three and a half years (1548–51), while the Earl of Salisbury spent £40,000 on Hatfield alone between 1604 and 1608.[6] Even aristocratic budgets couldn't cope with the expense of such building and the maintenance of huge numbers of servants.

Another reason for the decline of great households was the increasing cost of developing and maintaining your position at court. Throughout the sixteenth century it was impossible for a man to thrive without friends at court – 'like a hop without a pole', commented Burley. To be a figure of importance, you had to be at court yourself, and you also needed to be in favour with the monarch. There simply weren't enough jobs to go around and so without the monarch's favour you could find yourself bearing the considerable expenses involved in coming to court without garnering any of the benefits. This was a great problem as the costs of being at court were truly enormous.

One very important factor was clothing. You, the members of your family and even the servants who attended you all had to be well dressed. Being suitably attired for court became more and more expensive throughout the Elizabethan period and into the time of James I. Fashions became more extravagant and changed more frequently, and the amounts some people spent were extraordinary. Sir Henry Sidney's account for 1570–1 with Adam Bland, the queen's skinner, shows that he managed to run up an impressive bill of £66 6*s* 11*d* for fur linings alone. The furs included lynx, Spanish fox, black coney (a kind of rabbit) and lamb. In 1589 Bridget Manners, daughter of the Countess of Rutland, was sent from the Countess of Bedford's household, where she was completing her education, to join the royal household as a maid of honour. Her mother, fearing that her daughter was a little out of touch with fashion, spent no less than £200 updating Bridget's wardrobe.

Even the cost of accessories could be alarming. In 1583 Arthur Throckmorton, who was trying to build up a career at court, spent £6 on a set of eighteen gold buttons alone. Of course, some of this expense could be ascribed to mere vanity, but there was more to it than that. To be taken seriously at court you simply *had* to wear the latest fashions.

Then there were all the other incidental expenses of court life to take into consideration. There were presents to be bought for the monarch, and for anyone who could help you try to obtain jobs or favours, like the queen's ladies described above. The price of everything from food to accommodation was always high near the court, and those who came to court on their own business had to pay their way. Coming to court was a big gamble. If you were among the successful few, your outlay would be more than repaid by the rewards the monarch heaped upon you. If you were not, you could be bankrupted.

All these were reasons why the great lords no longer wanted to employ large numbers of servants, but there was another side to it. By the end of the sixteenth century gentlemen were not as willing as they once had been to join a great household, even if the work was available. One reason young men had been sent to such establishments was to gain an education, although this was by no means always paid for by the head of the household – the Earl of Northumberland's accounts show that such young men were often there 'at their friends' finding', that is to say, paid for by other people. By the late sixteenth century the introduction of schools like Eton and Westminster, plus a whole host of local grammar schools, meant that a good education could be obtained without access to a great household.

Equally, the need to wear a great man's livery faded as the private armies died out. Aristocrats remained people of considerable influence for many years to come, but making your allegiance too obvious was not necessarily wise. Anyone who was out of favour with the monarch was not really in a position to help your career too much. It was best to be able to be flexible, subtly changing your allegiance according to the political realities of the moment, than to openly wear someone's livery.

Another very important factor that contributed to the downfall of the great households was that, whatever the economics of the matter, great lords no longer wanted them. Impersonal grandeur, the mark of the great man in the Middle Ages and the early sixteenth century, was neither very comfortable nor particularly enjoyable. The Renaissance had emphasised the importance of the individual, and the aristocracy now wanted a more personal way of life. They wanted more comfort and privacy so that they could talk and behave as they wanted, instead of being on constant display before their household. If they wanted companionship, they could find it in London with men of their own rank, so that they no longer needed the company of employed gentlemen. The new emphasis on demonstrating wealth through fine architecture and elegant furnishings meant that you could put on a display fine enough to maintain your social position and live in comfort at the same time.

It was this new emphasis on privacy that led to a distance developing between a master and his servant. Once a personal servant stopped being a companion and became instead a person employed for purely practical reasons, the whole relationship changed. The link between personal service and opportunities in administration and the like was broken. There was no point in a gentleman being a lord's attendant if he could neither rise in his career nor be considered the lord's personal friend. In the same way employing lower-class personal attendants now made sense to the lord. He wouldn't have to pay them as well as a gentleman, and they wouldn't expect to be included in his private life.

The change can even be seen in architecture. In sixteenth-century houses separate staircases for servants' use did not exist. By the end of the seventeenth century they were becoming more common, and by the eighteenth century bells for summoning servants had been developed. A bell-pull in your private rooms rang a bell in the servants' quarters, so there was no longer any need to have a servant always within calling distance. At last you could have a private conversation without your servants overhearing. By this time masters and servants were truly living separate lives.

ONE

Goldsmiths, Fullers and Dyers
Learning your Trade in Tudor England

Tudor apprentices occupied a position somewhere between servant and family member. They lived in their master's house during their training in his craft and their master was, in effect, their parent for the duration of their apprenticeship. On the other hand, apprentices were expected to show a great deal of deference to their masters, even more than a child was expected to show to its parents at the time.

Apprentices varied considerably. At the top end were the children of the wealthy, apprenticed to prestigious trades such as that of goldsmith or mercer.[1] At the bottom end were orphaned paupers or those taken from poor families 'over burthened with children',[2] whose apprenticeships were organised by the parish and who were likely to be apprenticed to husbandry or housework. Their lot in life was generally to end up as farm labourers or menial domestic servants. It is unlikely that the parish children could expect to be treated like their masters' own.

The problem today is that many of the records of these apprentices no longer exist. Large numbers of records do survive, from indentures of individual apprentices to the rules of assorted guilds, but no complete record exists for any one area. For this reason we have a good idea of the lives of apprentices in general terms, but many specific details are lost. Part of the problem is that the same rules did not always apply across the whole country. Certain rules that were relevant to apprentices living in Carlisle or York cannot be assumed to have also applied to apprentices in London or Bristol. The Statute of Artificers (1562) went some way towards creating a national system but local customs still continued in most areas.

The situation is further complicated by the fact that the English apprenticeship system was not something that had been carefully planned from the beginning. It had grown up gradually, in accordance with the needs of the craft guilds.

A sixteenth-century guild was not just a trade organisation; it provided an important social club, a friendly society (members' widows and orphans could often expect help from the guild if necessary) and a bridge into politics, since the guilds often played a large part in running the town in which they worked. The social network provided by the guild offered you a busy social life and could also significantly improve your chances of success in business. Before the Reformation, guild members, or the guild priest if there was one, could even be relied on to pray for your soul after you died. Even after the religious upheavals the guild brethren would attend your funeral in force. There were often items such as a guild pall to add further magnificence to the event, at a time when a good funeral set a seal upon the achievements of your life. The guild, in short, was the centre of a businessman's life and it was no wonder that so many guild members left bequests of one kind or another to their guilds when they died, ranging from money to pay for feasts to embroidered cushions to beautify the guild's hall.

Guild membership was such an asset that people who didn't even follow the trade represented, or indeed any trade at all, were still keen to join, particularly the most important London guilds. The Masters of the guilds were smart businessmen who exploited this to the full, making a tidy profit from allowing wealthy men who did not follow the craft to join the guild all the same. The London Goldsmiths are a good example of this. In 1513 a Salisbury merchant who was not a goldsmith applied for membership, and the Wardens of the Goldsmiths' Company cheerfully stated in the minutes of their meeting that as he was not a goldsmith, they would 'take him for all they can get, and then admit him'. He ended up paying 40*s* entrance fee.[3] The Goldsmiths' Company also admitted a number of gentlemen members during the Tudor period. Contacts in the city, with their ability to raise money, were always useful to the gentlemen. Equally, contacts at court were necessary to the Goldsmiths in the days when the royal signature was vital for getting things done. Sir John Daunce (Thomas More's son-in-law) and Sir Francis Bryan (courtier and personal friend of Henry VIII) are just two examples of the Goldsmiths' gentlemen members.[4]

Guild membership of some kind was also a necessity for a businessman. You had to be a guild member – or be 'free of' the guild as the expression was – if you wanted to set up business in a particular town. The guilds had a long history of trying to limit competition. The difficult economic circumstances of the sixteenth century made them even more anxious to control trade in their area. Many of the guilds forbade 'foreigners', but their definition of the word was very narrow and might even include people from neighbouring districts. The Newcastle Adventurers' rules of 1575 refused to allow anyone from 'Tyndale, Riddesdale and Eskdale, or Levyn', all of which are in England and, by modern terms at least, not all that far from Newcastle, to become an apprentice.[5] Under such circumstances guild membership was vital if your career was to get off the ground at all, let alone thrive.

The guilds were keen on the apprenticeship system for a number of reasons. At first it was simply an effective way of allowing for the training of young people, and merely one way of several of becoming a member of a guild. In the thirteenth and fourteenth centuries you could join a guild whether or not you had served a formal apprenticeship, if you could prove yourself sufficiently skilled in your craft before competent judges. The London Fullers decreed in 1363 that they would allow any skilful workman to work at fulling, but if he were declared incompetent by the masters of the mystery, then he had either to become an apprentice and learn his business anew, or leave the trade. The Bristol Dyers and the Glovers of Hull were still doing this even at the end of the fifteenth century.[6] The only difference was that the entrance fee to the guild was higher than that paid by those who served their apprenticeship. In 1444 the Northampton Tailors charged 'strangers' an entry fee of 3*s* 4*d*, while those who had served their apprenticeships paid just 20*d*.

Gradually the guilds realised that by restricting entry they could do a great deal to control competition. Various barriers began to be put in the way of those who wanted to join the guilds by methods other than apprenticeship. In the 1460s the Exeter Merchant Tailors followed the general trend by raising the entrance fee for 'strangers' from 8 to a massive 20*s*. They could also be placed under other disadvantages. In the 1520s the Newcastle Merchant Adventurers forbade such guild members from taking apprentices, which, as we shall see, was a huge disadvantage.[7]

The guilds also became far more restrictive as to who could become an apprentice and the rules surrounding the whole matter became very complicated. Apprenticeship had started as an informal affair. Fathers and master craftsmen made their own arrangements as to how the details of the agreement between them should work. But by the sixteenth century it was a public affair involving the whole guild and it became standard for the official enrolment of the boy's indentures to take place before the full court of the guild, where he could be presented to the masters and wardens. In the same way, when he finished his time, his formal acceptance into the guild also took place in public.

By the sixteenth century organising an apprenticeship for your child must have been every bit as fraught as finding the right school today. The first thing you had to consider was whether or not your child was eligible, as there were a number of qualifications to be met. Again, the information that has survived comes from different areas of the country and not all of the rules may have been applicable everywhere. Still, the extant information gives a good idea of the kind of regulations that had to be met. Some of the higher-status guilds required educational qualifications. The Goldsmiths refused apprenticeship to those who couldn't read or write, and in 1483 one master was fined for taking an illiterate apprentice.[8] In 1487 there was a strange case, when a goldsmith took on an apprentice who had already learnt the craft at Banbury. The boy was skilled in engraving all kinds of letters so the master, not unreasonably, assumed that he could read and write. It was only later that he realised that the apprentice was illiterate.[9]

Many of the guilds refused to take foreigners and this does seem to have been a common restriction. Certainly in Henry VIII's reign an act was passed stating that strangers born outside England were only permitted to take English apprentices, thus excluding their own countrymen who might by this means set up trade in England. Age was another restriction. The Newcastle Merchant Adventurers wouldn't take boys under sixteen and the Norwich Weavers forbade apprentices under the age of fourteen.[10] The Newcastle Merchant Adventurers refused to take illegitimate children, their rules of 1513 stating that 'No bastard shall be free of this Feloship, though he have served and bene vii yer apprentyce'. Several companies also refused to take any apprentices who were deformed in any way. The London Skinners and Mercers both refused entry to such boys, while the Leathersellers' rules of 1467 insisted that boys were to be presented to the company before being accepted to see if they were 'of clenly feture and not deformed in his visage nor in noe other parts of limbs of his body'. Marriage was also a bar to apprenticeship – at Norwich this stipulation was frequently made by the guilds long before the Statute of Artificers made it law for the whole country in 1562.

Having discovered that your son was eligible to be apprenticed, you then had to check that the master you had chosen for him was officially entitled to take apprentices. If a boy was bound apprentice to a man who was not qualified to be a master of his craft, then the guilds might not sanction the agreement and the boy would have to search for a new master. The worst situation of all arose when a boy only discovered that his master was not qualified at the end of his indentures, in which case the apprentice might find himself refused entry to the guild.

The most obvious qualification was that the master had to be a freeman of the guild and of the town or city in which he lived. In many cases he also had to own property worth a certain amount of money. The Mercers, for example, stated in 1504 that a master must own £100 worth of stock or other goods.[11] This must have been a practical rule to some extent, ensuring that the boy was being bound to a secure business that would last out his time. The Skinners too stated that men who wished to take apprentices must prove themselves able to teach, employ and maintain them. At Coventry a master had to be quit of any money owing to the guild before taking on an apprentice, while in Carlisle he had to be married.

The right to take apprentices was vital to most masters as they provided a cheap workforce. The master was usually expected to feed, clothe and house his apprentices, but he didn't have to pay them. It was usual to give them some kind of lump sum at the end of their apprenticeship to help set them up in business and sometimes apprentices were given small amounts of what was, in practical terms, pocket money but that was all. The idea was that the apprentice gave his labour in return for the time invested in him by his master in teaching him his trade.

Apprentices were so useful to their masters that the right to their services was a saleable commodity. Some masters sold their apprentices on to other masters (known as 'custom of sale' or 'turnover') or even sold a portion of their term back to the apprentice himself. The latter practice in particular was not encouraged, as it could lead to apprentices finishing their training before they were fully qualified. As early as 1368 the London Goldsmiths had rules on the matter: 'If any apprentice buys his term or part thereof or if his master pardons him his term or releases him, he shall not hold shop during his term nor be enfranchised, nor do work in private places but be bound freeman of the mystrey unless by assent of the Wardens and with a voluntary contribution.'[12]

Turnover was a different matter. The guilds were very strict in limiting the number of apprentices that a master was allowed to take, partly because a master with too many apprentices would not be able to teach any of them satisfactorily, and partly because the guilds were keen to limit their membership and therefore reduce competition. Thus they kept a close eye on the number of apprentices in training generally. For this reason men who had the right to take apprentices but chose not to do so could take on their allocated number of boys and then 'turn them over' to another master who wanted more apprentices than he was officially allowed. The whole matter was carefully regulated. The Goldsmiths' rules of 1384 state that: 'No one shall sell an apprentice the remainder of his term or to any other person of any other trade, but only to a freeman of the same trade and of the same city, and that the seller shall pay half of what he receives to the alms.'[13]

It certainly could be a profitable business. The London Merchant Tailors' accounts show a fine levied in 1547 on Harry Whytehorne, a master who sold his apprentice without leave. The fine was for 8*s* 10*d*, which is stated as being a third part of the profit he gained from the deal, thus making a fine profit of 17*s* 8*d*. When you consider that the Johnson family (see below) were paying their cook 21*s* a year in 1550, this was no small sum.

There were obviously occasions when masters were forced to give up their apprentices whether they liked it or not. If they went bankrupt, or if they became unable to employ the apprentice because of illness or death, then the apprentice would either serve out his time with the master's widow or heir, or be transferred to some other suitable master. This again was supervised by the guild and a small sum was charged for the process.

To make matters more confusing, the number of apprentices a master was allowed to take varied from city to city and from trade to trade. The Exeter Tailors did not grant more than one apprentice per master without special permission. The Newcastle Merchant Adventurers were also allowed only one, although they were permitted to take a new apprentice a year or two before the old one came to the end of his term, to ensure continuity of support in their work. The Skinners permitted an old master to have four apprentices over seven years, a warden could have three and an ordinary master two over the same period.[14]

Assuming that both the boy and his master were qualified, indentures would be drawn up and signed by both parties. The exact wording of the indentures varied, but the terms were fairly general. The boy had to promise to keep his master's secrets, to neither intend nor do any harm to his master or his business, to look after his master's goods and neither sell them nor lend them to anyone without permission. Other promises the boy made went far beyond the bounds of most employment agreements today: he would not get involved in gambling, he would not go to ale houses 'or any suspect places' without his master's permission, and also would not 'use or occupye lecher or fornycacion', especially in his master's house. He also promised not to marry during his apprenticeship without his master's permission. In return for the apprentice's labour, the master usually promised to provide clothes (often described as both woollen and linen clothing, meaning both top and underclothes), bedding, food, drink and often washing. The agreement would be written out twice, then the parchment on which it was written would be cut in two by a jagged line, the 'indenture'. The master would have one half and the apprentice the other. The exact shape of the cut would be unique to each document, to prevent fraud.

Apprentices were frequently sent far from home. This was particularly the case in London, which offered the best career opportunities and so drew apprentices from all over the country, but even smaller towns drew apprentices from a surprisingly wide area. The sixteenth-century records for Kingston upon Thames show that some apprentices came from Southampton, Hever (in Kent), Shropshire, Exeter, Westmorland, Anglesey, Nottingham and Ripon, to name just a few of the more distant places.[15] This meant that there was an intensely personal aspect to apprenticeship, as the master and his wife took the place of the apprentice's parents. Under these circumstances, you can understand why in Carlisle (and perhaps in other places too) a master had to be married before he was allowed to take apprentices. He had to provide not just a business environment but a home for them, and was expected not only to teach the boy his trade, but also to ensure that he learnt good manners and behaved well.

Rigid discipline was imposed and a great deal of corporal punishment was used. The apprentice was, of course, less important than his master and was given every opportunity to learn this. A boy who felt that this was being taken too far had to prove that his treatment was more severe than was reasonable. How severe punishment could be is demonstrated by the case of a goldsmith's apprentice who felt that having his mistress run a needle through his thumb was 'ayens all reison and laweful demeanyng'.[16]

The attitude expected from an apprentice, at least in theory, can be seen from the preamble to an act passed by the Newcastle Merchant Adventurers in 1584. The act was aimed at controlling what the apprentices wore, but the preamble starts by stating how apprentices ought to behave, and how in the past the masters insisted on correct behaviour:

> Whereas in the educacion and bringing up of apprentices, no little regarde and studye hathe remaind in our elders, that like as the dewtie of the apprentize was entructed him to God, so was the same not forgotten, what reverence ought to be doone to the maister and mystress, what obedyence to there superiours, what honest loove unto there equallds, what temperaunce in meate, drynche and apparell . . .[17]

While it is difficult to believe that the Newcastle apprentices in earlier times were indeed such paragons of virtue, the point is clear. Due respect and moderate habits were expected. But showing suitable respect was only the beginning. Apprentices had to go beyond this and show due courtesy. Courtesy meant behaving correctly in all circumstances, not only as a way of gaining respect in the world, but also of showing yourself to be doing your duty as a Christian. This is why etiquette books of the time cheerfully mix instructions to pray regularly with explanations of correct etiquette. It was all seen as part of the same idea.[18]

The general aim was an air of quiet dignity. In the presence of superiors, this showed suitable respect. In the presence of inferiors, it showed authority. Equally, such restraint indicated that you were avoiding sins such as anger. This level of dignity was also very useful for someone in business. It suggested that they could be relied upon to keep their own counsel if necessary. Such behaviour was considered so important that it was also enforced on adults who were full guild members, and not just on apprentices. Guild records are peppered with accounts of guild members brought before the wardens for quarrelling loudly in the guildhall, particularly if the offence was committed in the presence of the wardens of the company. The Goldsmiths even record the case of Robert Sayles and Thomas Greene, whose wives were evidently enemies who quarrelled in public: 'The husband of her who begins the difference shall forfeit on each occasion 3 shillings and 4 pence to the alms of St Dunstan [the patron saint of the goldsmiths], and that if the wife first abused replies in like language, her husband shall pay each time to the same alms 20 pence . . .'[19] Such behaviour was not to be tolerated in public.

All of this helps to explain the apprentices' promises regarding their social lives. A particular master might have a puritanical streak, but in general it doesn't seem that anyone objected to apprentices having a good night out. What they did object to was waste. The preamble to the Newcastle Act, mentioned above, goes on to complain about the behaviour of modern apprentices: 'for never amonge apprentices, and chiefelye of this said Feoloshipe, hath bene more abused and inconvenyent behavour than ys of theim at this daye frequented for what dyseng, cardeng and mumming, what typlinge, daunseng and brasenge of harlots . . .'.

Of course the complaints were partly the perpetual moans of the older generation against the younger, but a wise sixteenth-century apprentice had to think carefully about his reputation. A man who wasted his money on dice, cards, drinking and prostitutes was hardly likely to be a big success in business. And once his time was finished, an apprentice would be looking for a wife, preferably one with a good dowry. Parents and guardians didn't like giving daughters to men likely to waste their hard-earned dowry money.

One London draper directed in his will that his daughters were to be married to 'suche sadde and discrete persones . . . as seem convenyent and profitable'.[20] A master who insisted that his apprentice keep his social life within certain limits was doing him a favour.

Given that the relationship between master and apprentice was so complex, it is not surprising that a number of conflicts developed. One difficult area was football, a subject that can still be controversial today. Sixteenth-century football was nothing like the modern game. It simply consisted of two teams, of no particular size, who had to get a football (or sometimes some other object) from one chosen place to another chosen place, which would be different for each team. There were virtually no rules and anything could, and did, happen. Broken bones and even deaths were caused by the game. The apprentices, like most young men of the day, were keen to join in the fun. The authorities, and anyone who owned property likely to be damaged, were of a different mind. Sir Thomas Elyot, in his *Boke named the Governor*, which discussed the education of the well-bred young boy, described it as 'a beastly fury and extreme violence; whereof proceedeth hurt, and consequently rancour and malice do remain with them that be wounded'. The Shoemakers of Carlisle heartily agreed and declared: 'Item: it is fully condiscended and agreed upon by the fellowship of this gyld that no journeyman or apprentice shall make any foot balle to sell or play withal without consent and knowledge of his or their maisters and that they shall not play at football within the liberties of this cittie.'[21]

Football was only the beginning. A far greater area of conflict was clothing. The precise definition of 'suitable clothing' can still be a bone of contention in families today, but in Tudor times it was a far more sensitive issue. This was a status conscious age and the way most people showed their status was through their clothing. It was such an important area at this time that there were even 'Acts of Apparel' that controlled what people were allowed to wear. Henry VIII, Mary I and Elizabeth all passed such laws. They were hard to enforce, though, as those rich enough to flaunt them were often so influential that few people dared risk offending them by criticising their clothes. In 1580 the Lord Mayor of London himself displeased Mr Hewson, the son-in-law of the Lord Chief Baron, when he told him off (apparently in a friendly fashion) for wearing a large ruff 'against her Majesty's proclamation'.[22] Mr Hewson was unimpressed, and told the Lord Mayor so in no uncertain terms. The Lord Mayor, feeling that his dignity was threatened, tried to enforce the law against Mr Hewson, but ended up falling foul of the Lord Chief Baron himself, who felt that a mere Lord Mayor should not criticise his son-in-law.

If such dignitaries as the Lord Mayor of London and the Lord Chief Baron could fall out over matters of dress, then apprentices were hardly likely to be able to avoid the issue. An apprentice who chose to dress more fashionably or more expensively than his master thought suitable was seen as openly defying his master, a state of affairs that could hardly be allowed to continue. The Newcastle Act of 1554, the preamble to which has already been discussed, was largely concerned with apprentices' clothing. It professes horror at the excesses of the apprentices' dress: 'what garded cotes, jagged hose, lyned with silke, and cutt shoes', it complains. Such clothes were vastly expensive at the time, and were more suggestive of a rich gentleman's son than a humble apprentice. Of course, that was the problem. Some of the apprentices *were* rich gentlemen's sons, who not only had the money to dress expensively but also felt that they had every right to do so. The mayor, aldermen and sheriffs felt differently about this threat to the social order. The act was duly set in place, giving the authorities the power to make any rules they chose over how apprentices should dress. Masters of offending apprentices were to be fined, while the apprentices themselves were to forfeit the time they had served if they were caught breaking the rules. However, the apprentices were not about to give up their finery and meekly comply. In 1603 a prison was established in Newcastle where offending apprentices could be sent until the Governor, or their master or mistress, let them out. Further similar acts were passed in 1649 and 1697, indicating that the problem was never really solved.

There were other offences that an apprentice could commit. Guild records show them being punished for various misdemeanours, some of which, as you might expect, seem more the product of youthful high spirits than of anything else. The Goldsmiths' records tell of one Thomas Atkinson, apprentice, who was punished before Alderman Bowes and the wardens in 1557 'for abuse of Thomas Medcalf, and for making an horned head upon his door set between the letters of his name, and for other villainies'.[23] Horns were the symbol of the cuckold so Master Atkinson's actions were particularly insolent. But not all offences can be so easily dismissed. In the same year there was a rather more serious incident involving a 'naughty confederacy of certain unthrifty apprentices in Cheap, which had deceived their masters, and with their goods had maintained riots and banquets'.[24] Whatever their offence, apprentices were punished in public, before the wardens, as a warning to others. Their exact punishment is often not stated, but in 1535 the Goldsmiths instructed 'disguised persons' to beat one apprentice with rods in their hall.[25]

The picture of apprenticeship so far is rather bleak, but in fact it need not necessarily have been so. Most of our information comes from guild records, so most apprentices appear merely as names mentioned when they are first apprenticed and again when they take up their freedom at the end of their time. The others tend to appear only because they got into trouble, or because they were in some way dissatisfied with their treatment. The apprentices who were anything from satisfied to completely happy with their masters simply do not appear in the records.

Apprentices were not necessarily helpless either. They were able to complain if they felt they were not being treated well, and masters were fined for taking advantage. The Merchant Tailors fined a master 5*s* for beating his apprentice unlawfully, while another was fined 10*s* for 'clothing his boy badly to the great disgrace of the misteries'. Sixteenth-century sensibilities about clothes did not always work against the apprentices.[26]

The guilds did not forget about the apprentices, even if they do not appear in their records. In order to check that guild rules were being followed and standards of workmanship maintained, the guilds employed searchers, whose job was to visit the guild members' workshops unannounced. In doing so, they could also ensure that the apprentices were treated properly. The guild's own interests and those of the apprentices often coincided. For example, the guilds wanted well-trained apprentices, so anyone who felt that their master was failing to teach them their trade properly could expect a sympathetic response, provided they could prove their case. In the same way apprentices were protected from overwork as the guilds did not want anyone to work by candlelight, as it was hard to produce good work in such uncertain light. As the searchers didn't work after dark, there was the very real possibility that work or business done by night would be deliberately fraudulent in some way. In 1599 the Goldsmiths had dealings with a certain John Scacie, evidently a less-than-honest member of his trade, who was found guilty of selling sub-standard goldware. Among the many charges against him was that of 'selling the wares by candlelight', which was against the company's ordinances 'both ancient and modern'.[27]

Masters and apprentices were also perfectly capable of reaching sensible compromises on some issues. Generally speaking, apprentices were not allowed to trade on their own account, as this would be seen as harming their master's business. But this could result in problems in trades based around buying and selling, such as that of merchant adventurer, where a boy could hardly learn anything without trading on his own account. The Newcastle Adventurers got round the problem by allowing apprentices to trade on their own account after five years' service and only with stock to the value of 5 marks.[28]

This need for flexibility brings us to another vital but often overlooked aspect of apprenticeship, the personal relationship between master and apprentice. As we have already seen, a master took the place of an apprentice's father and supervised his whole life. However competent the master or good the apprentice, if the two really disliked each other it must have been hard to make the agreement work. Sadly we have practically no personal records to throw light on this important matter. Fortunately some letters do survive from the Johnson family, who were merchants at the Staple in Calais in the mid-fifteenth century. Their experiences with apprentices give an idea of how the arrangement could be affected, for both better and worse, by the simple matter of whether or not they got on with their apprentices.

The Staple merchants were generally well-to-do and the Johnsons were no exception. They had a country house, Glapthorne Manor, where a new apprentice, William Pratt, was sent in 1545. Things started badly for he immediately decided that the food he was given was not good enough, and there was not enough of it. He wrote home miserably to his mother, who promptly went and complained to his master John Johnson, who was in London at the time. This left John Johnson with the uncomfortable task of writing to his wife Sabine to explain the problem. Here is some of the letter:

> Your young gentleman, Master Pratt, hath complained by his letter to his mother that he lacketh both meat and drink, as well his breakfasts, as also at meals not sufficient. All your menservants have been of counsel with him, for they be of no less opinion, declaring that your bread is not good enough for dogs, and drink so evil that they cannot drink it, but are fain when they go into the town to drink to their dinners. If you know they complain with cause, I pray you see it amended: if they complain without cause, let them seek new masters and boarding . . .

Needless to say, Sabine was not impressed. She looked into the matter and decided that Master Pratt was complaining for no reason. Here is part of her reply:

> As for Master Pratt's complaint, I can find nobody in fault but himself, and he doth deny that he did write any such things but lack of meat and drink. If three meals a day in winter and four in summer be not sufficient, I would his mother had him, that she

> might feed him every hour. I will have all my house to say with me that he had his breakfast, his dinner and supper all well eaten . . .[29]

Obviously all was not well between Master Pratt and the Johnsons. But things seem to have got worse, so that at Christmas William was left in London with John's brother Otwell, while John went home to Glapthorne. Otwell soon discovered that William disliked John intensely. As John's business partner, he decided that it would be best if William found himself another master. Here is part of his letter explaining matters to John:

> Master Pratt, your man that was, will dwell no more with you, unless you will be his servant, for he can in nowise find in his heart to serve you, nor never did hitherto with any good-will, as he hath now plainly declared to me, and I have done the same again in his behalf to his father and mother. All that he hath done heretofore hath been counterfeited, and without any manner of love towards you or your wife, being in fear of his friends' displeasure . . .[30]

As far as we can tell, the only problem was one of clashing personalities, but it was enough to cause the end of Master Pratt's apprenticeship.

The Johnsons also had problems with other apprentices. One, John Kele, turned out just not to be merchant material, and was eventually sent home to his father. They seem to have been very fond of another apprentice, Henry Johnson (who wasn't related to them), but unfortunately the boy died in the autumn of 1545. He died of suspected plague, but in Otwell's arms. He was the second of the Johnsons' apprentices to die of plague. Another, Thomas Holland, had died of it the year before.

Not all the Johnsons' apprentices proved problematic. Far more successful was Richard Sandell, the son of an Essex sheep farmer. He developed a very good relationship with Otwell and his wife Maria, with whom he lived. He was also a great asset to the business for many years before he left to set up on his own. Perhaps their most interesting apprentice was William Tupholme, whose father was Mayor of Boston. He started off being something of a problem to the Johnsons, but fortunately he was no repeat of William Pratt. He was an only son, but his father was anxious for him not only to do well but also to behave himself. At first he seems to have been anything but a promising young man. A surviving letter to him from his father begs 'To see you do well, it is the chief care that I have in my mind, wherefore endeavour yourself in all your master's business, that I may once have a loving letter from your master (in your praise), the which were a great pleasure to me to hear of. . . .' Despite his bad beginning William did eventually settle in and went on to become a wealthy merchant himself, operating from his home town of Boston.

It was helpful if you did get on with your master as apprenticeship was a long business. The length of the indentures varied, but it was generally at least seven years. In some of the highly skilled trades and those which involved a great deal of business acumen, this was quite reasonable. Boys generally started their apprenticeship around the age of fourteen, so by their early twenties they could have learnt enough to become independent traders. However, the length of service was often longer than was really required to learn the job. The Newcastle Merchant Adventurers insisted on ten years' service by the middle of the sixteenth century, as did the Goldsmiths. This had nothing to do with the needs of the apprentices, but was an attempt to restrict the numbers of people who had served their time. The Adventurers stated quite openly that 'the numbers of this Felowship is so augmented, and dayly doith increas, tht if spedie remedie in this case were not provided it would be the utter destruction of this hole Felowship'.[31]

Another reason for the extension of indentures was that over-hasty marriage at too young an age was thought to be exacerbating the economic problems of the time. The Statute of Artificers stated that no one should come out of their indentures before the age of twenty-four. Apprentices were not allowed to marry during their time, so this was one way of stopping early marriage.

If you managed to survive to the age of twenty-four without seriously offending either your master or the guild, there were still hurdles to be cleared before you gained your freedom. One was the completion of your masterpiece, an example of your craft which would prove your skill to the wardens of your guild. The idea of a masterpiece was by no means universal in the sixteenth century, but it was not uncommon. The 1571 ordinances of the Goldsmiths' Company state that young men must not set up for themselves until they have made their masterpieces. The exact details of such a masterpiece are not known, but this could be more of a barrier than first appears. The production of such an item might cost a great deal of money and take a long time. Considering that apprentices didn't earn any money, this could have posed a problem for those whose parents couldn't afford to pay for materials.

Even after your masterpiece was completed, if one was required, there were other matters to consider, particularly the fees that had to be paid. In theory, the fees for joining the guild were set by statute at 3*s* 4*d* but in practice they were much higher. Some guilds also insisted on new members providing gifts, or paying for dinners and other such things, so that the cost of taking up your freedom even after serving your time was considerable. And even when you had joined the guild, you also had to pay for the freedom of your particular town or city before you could set up business.

The apprentice could expect some money from his master at the end of his time, but it was nothing like enough to set him up in business. The amount varied enormously and was part of the agreement made between the apprentice and his master at the beginning of his time. Sometimes the apprentice was given just money but some were also paid at least partly in tools. In Kingston upon Thames Jeffray Hewett, who was apprenticed to Thomas Creswell, wheelwright, in 1582 could expect 40*s* plus an axe, auger, adze, burr and shave, which were all tools of his trade. Christopher Bickerdyke, who was apprenticed to a Kingston mercer in 1585, could expect only 20*s* at the end of his apprenticeship. William Combes, apprenticed in 1580 to a carpenter, was promised wages of

20*s* and an additional 6*s* 8*d* in either money or tools, at his own choosing.[32]

Given this situation there were not many young men who could afford to set up as a master immediately after gaining their freedom. It was an expensive business to get a set of tools together, and then you still had to establish a shop or booth where you could work. Many had no choice but to work as journeymen for a master until they had saved some money and there must have been plenty who never managed to become a master at all.

So far it is easy to get the impression that all apprentices, apart from a few bound to learn housework, were all boys. In fact girls were bound apprentice in the sixteenth century and women could play an active part in business, but that is not to say that the Tudors believed in equal opportunities. Apprenticeship was certainly never the rule for girls, as it was for boys. However, despite the fact that they were vastly outnumbered by boys, there were enough girl apprentices for them to be specifically mentioned in an act of 1389 forbidding labourers to apprentice their children. In 1413 the Corporation of London fixed the fees of both male and female apprentices, so that female apprentices must have been common enough to warrant their inclusion in the legislation.[33] However, closer study shows how small their numbers actually were. Between 1542 and 1552 only 3 per cent of guild apprentices in Bristol were girls.[34]

The difficult financial climate seems to have encouraged the guilds generally to try to exclude people from trade in an effort to reduce competition. In 1563 the Goldsmiths passed an ordinance forbidding the taking of more apprentices, as the trade was already overstocked.[35] In fact, they did not stop doing so, as such a move was hardly practical, but it does show the feeling of the times. In the circumstances it is not surprising that attempts were made to keep women from taking any part in business. After all, women played no official part in running the guilds and were therefore powerless to stop any moves made against them. Ironically, it is the rules forbidding women's employment that show that they were involved.

In 1590 Andrew Bowyer, a pewterer, was fined for employing a woman to engrave his pewter. Despite this, he went on employing the woman and was fined a second time. In 1562 the Bristol Weavers forbade women and aliens to work, complaining that men were employing their wives and daughters to work their looms, or were allowing others to employ them. The official excuse for forbidding them to work was that it left men, who could serve the king in his wars, 'vagrant and unemployed'.[36]

This is not to say that women had no part in business in Tudor times. From the regulations it seems that women often did have the skills to work at a trade, but were only allowed to exercise them if they were working on their family's behalf. Wives and daughters must have been useful employees. It was difficult to employ skilled labour on a short-term basis, so if an unexpectedly large order came to your business, or if at certain times of year extra help was needed, the women of the family came in handy. It does seem too that many wives understood their husband's business, as a widow was allowed to carry on her deceased husband's business if she so chose. She could even continue to train apprentices. What she couldn't do was set up on her own behalf and trade on equal terms with the men.

This was life for the wealthy or reasonably well-off apprentice, male or female. They usually had concerned parents who were interested in their welfare, and were apprenticed to learn established trades in the houses of master craftsmen. But this was by no means the case with all sixteenth-century apprentices. Poor children had long been apprenticed to 'husbandry' (agriculture) and 'huswifery' (housework) and working in either of these two areas was very different from being an apprentice to a prestige trade (see chapter 3). The situation changed further in the second half of the sixteenth century when legislation was brought in making apprenticeship for young people universal, at least in theory.

The popular view of the reign of Elizabeth I is one of prosperity and splendour, but this is largely the result of the Tudor family's gift for clever propaganda and has little to do with reality. The second half of the sixteenth century was a difficult time financially, with a great deal of inflation and unemployment. The unemployed often went wandering around the country in search of work, leading to fears of 'wandering rogues and vagabonds'.[37] Nobody was exactly sure what to do about them. A number of laws were passed during this period trying to deal with the problem, but the two major pieces of legislation were the Statute of Artificers of 1562 and the Poor Law of 1601.

The Statute of Artificers recognised the fact that employment in general was hedged about by a whole host of differing laws and regulations. The intention was to codify the law, so it didn't so much introduce new ideas as enforce old ones. It was also an attempt to stabilise the employment situation. It tried to stop employees leaving on a whim, and employers dismissing their staff for no real reason. It tried to control wages, which were rising at a time of inflation. It also aimed at ensuring that all young people who needed a trade in order to live should be apprenticed. This latter point was further enforced by the Poor Law, which included not only orphaned children but also 'the children of all such whose parents shall not by the said church-wardens and overseers . . . be thought able to keep and maintain their children'.

Sadly there are no personal records left by any of these children, so we know little of their working conditions. However, the Statute of Artificers regulates the hours that 'artificers and labourers' were supposed to work. Between mid-March and mid-September they were to start 'at or before' five in the morning and work until seven or eight at night. They were allowed two and a half hours for meals and 'drinking' (the Tudor equivalent of a tea-break), with half an hour for breakfast, an hour for dinner and half an hour per drink break. From the middle of May until the middle of August they also got a half-hour break to sleep, although the act says this should be included in the two and a half hours. Between mid-September and mid-March, when of course the days were shorter, they were to work from dawn until nightfall, and would be fined 1*d* for every hour's absence if they didn't turn up for work.

It all sounds reasonable, but the problem is that no measures were put in place to enforce the act. In reality, child apprentices must have been almost entirely at the mercy of their masters. The parish overseers were under considerable pressure to keep the poor rate as low as possible, and doubtless would not have asked too many questions of someone prepared to take on a poor child. This is not to say that they were all exploited, of course, but they must have been very vulnerable. According to the Statute of Artificers any apprentice had the right to go to a local justice of the peace if they felt they were being mistreated. If the apprentice won his case, he could then be discharged from his master. However, there was no provision for any sort of compensation so even then the apprentice might be left with no real trade and nowhere to go. Even an exceptionally gifted poor child would have few opportunities unless some rich patron took an interest in them for some reason. The cost of apprenticeship to a more profitable trade than farming would have been far more than the parish would have been prepared to pay.

A successful apprenticeship in the sixteenth century relied therefore on a number of factors. It depended not only on finding the right trade for a child's skills, but also on finding the right master. As the Johnsons found out, the wrong apprentice could cause considerable difficulty both in the business and at home. As Sabine Johnson's brother Ambrose wrote: 'A good servant is the blessing of the Lord'. Doubtless the apprentices felt the same way about a good master.

TWO

John Blank Comes to Court
Black Servants in Sixteenth-century England

By Elizabeth I's reign the number of black servants in England was rising. Unfortunately there are no personal records written by any of these people relating their experiences in their own words, so what they thought of their lot in service is impossible to know. Equally, what the white community made of them can only be seen through Elizabethan books published about Africa and odd references to black people in accounts, court records and legislation.

The most obvious way that many black servants came to England was through the slave trade. In the sixteenth century England was not an important slave-trading nation. The Spanish and the Portuguese were the European countries most involved in the trade, as they maintained large overseas colonies where slave labour was required. The English interest in Africa was centred around trading for luxuries such as gold, pepper and ivory. In 1554 John Locke, an English merchant who traded with Africa, brought some slaves from West Africa to England and sold them as household servants.[1] This seems to have started a fashion for wealthy families to keep a few black slaves in their household as exotic curiosities. Lady Raleigh, wife of Sir Walter, was one such early slave owner.[2] By the end of the seventeenth century having black slaves in your household had become a necessity for anyone who wanted to be seen as stylish, but the fashion had started over a hundred years before.

Sir John Hawkins was the first Englishman to take part in the highly profitable triangular trade which took African slaves to the Caribbean and America. His first voyage took place in 1562/3[3] and he acquired about three hundred slaves from the Guinea coast. Some he bought from African merchants, some he stole from Portuguese traders and others he simply seized. He took them to Hispaniola (now Haiti and the Dominican Republic) and sold them to the Spaniards there for £10,000-worth of pearls, hides, sugar and ginger, making himself a profit of about 12 per cent. It is of note that nobody in England seems to have been critical of Hawkins. Elizabeth I herself lent him for his next voyage the 600-ton *Jesus of Lubeck*, a ship that had been bought for the English navy at the cost of £4,000 – this was definite royal encouragement. Elizabeth, of course, never turned down a chance to make money. Hawkins himself was proud of his slaving activities. Indeed, his new coat of arms included three black men shackled with slave collars, with a crest of another black man's head.

From the 1570s onwards black slaves were regularly brought to England. It is hard to know what exactly happened when they got here, as the evidence is fragmentary. For example, an assessment of 'strangers' (foreigners) in All Hallows parish, Tower Ward, in about 1598 mentions four black people – Clare who lived at Widow Stoke's, Maria at Olyver Kynmar's, Jesse (or perhaps Lewse) at Mr Milton's, and Marea at Mr Wood's. All we know is that they existed. The area of London in which they lived was certainly not a fashionable, wealthy one, so presumably they were not being kept simply as status symbols but must have been earning their livings somehow. We have no way of knowing if they were treated as servants, being paid for their work and treated like their white counterparts, or if they were slaves.[4]

By the end of the sixteenth century there were enough black people in Britain to warrant the attention of the queen herself. Unfortunately for them, it was the kind of attention they could well have done without. On 11 June 1596 Elizabeth sent an open letter to the Lord Mayor of London and his aldermen and to the mayors and sheriffs throughout England: 'Her Majestie understanding that there are of late divers blackmoores brought into this realme, of which kinde of people there are already too manie . . . Her Majesty's pleasure therefore ys that those kinde of people should be sent forth of the lande.'[5]

But it does not seem to represent an attempt to throw out the entire black population of England, since the letter goes on to specify 'those blackmoores' brought by Sir Thomas Baskervile in his last voyage. The letter was followed a week later by an open warrant to the Lord Mayor of London, vice-admirals, mayors and other public officers informing them that a German merchant called Casper van Senden had arranged for the release of eighty-nine English prisoners from the Spanish and Portuguese. In return he was to be given eighty-nine black slaves. The government merely confiscated the required number from their owners and handed them over.

The proclamation sheds light on an unpleasant side of Elizabethan life: xenophobia. The difficult economic circumstances of the late sixteenth century had caused considerable unemployment and in some quarters it was felt that importing black slaves could only make the problem worse. In 1601 Elizabeth issued another proclamation, and this time she *was* trying to remove the entire black population from England, again via Casper van Senden. The reasons given have a horribly modern feel to them: 'the great number of Negroes and blackamoors are fostered and powered here, to the great annoyance of her own liege people which covet the relief which their people consume'. The Elizabethans, just like many others before and after them, found it easy to blame a minority for a very complicated social problem. However, the proclamation failed and the black population stayed.

Some of the black population of England in Elizabeth's time were visitors rather than permanent residents. Five of the most interesting ones we know of came from Shama, on the coast of Ghana, in 1555. They may or may not have been slaves, but they came here not as servants but as language students. The English were having problems getting into the African trade, which was controlled by the Portuguese. Naturally the Portuguese were keen to keep the trade for themselves and worked hard to exclude any foreigners who tried to take a share. In order to find their way into the market the English needed Africans who could both speak English and represent English interests among the native groups with whom they hoped to trade.

The five were brought to London but after a few months three of them went home again with a London merchant named William Towerson, whose actions were evidently not entirely altruistic as the three Africans were soon persuading their fellows that it was safe to go on board the English ships for trading purposes. In his *Principall Navigations* Richard Hackluyt describes the welcome the men received when they arrived home: 'the men of the towne wept for you, when thye saw them, and at Sham itself one of them was greeted by an aunt, another by a sister-in-law and there ladies received them with much ioy, and so did all the rest of the people, as if they had bene their naturall brethren'. No doubt the men's relatives had thought that once the men had left on a ship for England, they would never return to Africa.[6]

Black servants could also be found in even the highest levels of society owing to the fashion for their services in court circles. At the English court there was a black trumpeter, recorded in the accounts of the Treasurer of the Chamber as John Blank (from Blanc, meaning white, and presumably a nickname), who worked for both Henry VII and Henry VIII. He was paid 8*d* a day, so was hardly a slave. He is probably the black trumpeter who appears on the Westminster Tournament Roll of 1511, which depicts the tournament held by Henry VIII to celebrate the birth of his son, the short-lived Prince Henry.

The English court continued its fascination with black people throughout the sixteenth century. Clearly they were seen as somehow exotic, as a number of court entertainments were based around them, although they were usually played by white people in black make-up. In 1510, at another court entertainment, Henry and the Earl of Essex appeared 'appareled of Turkey fashion' with two torch-bearers with their faces blackened, while at least two of the court ladies taking part were dressed in the Egyptian style, with blacked faces, necks and arms. Similarly Edward VI took part in a Shrovetide masque in 1548 as a young moor, wearing elbow-length black velvet gloves and black leather hose.[7]

Elizabeth I, as far as we know, never appeared in black make-up, but she certainly followed the fashion for employing black servants. In 1577 the Lord Chamberlain's accounts show a very fine Gascon coat being made for a 'lytle Blackamore'. It was made of silk taffeta and tinsel (a thin cloth of sparkling gold or silver) and decorated with ribbons. There is also a picture of what is obviously a courtly entertainment, although exactly when and where is unknown, at which a group of black musicians can be seen playing. It is thought to have been painted by Marcus Gheeraerts the Elder in about 1575.[8]

The sixteenth-century Scots court was even more enthusiastic about black entertainers. King James IV had a number of black servants, especially musicians. There were also several black women servants, including one who was an attendant to Queen Margaret, Henry VIII's sister. The poet William Dunbar describes an elaborate court entertainment in which the king himself played the Black Knight, who championed the black lady (who actually was black, rather than a white lady wearing make-up). She was provided with an impressive gown which cost a princely £29, and she made a remarkable exit at the end of the forty-day tournament when a conjuror made a cloud descend from the roof of the banqueting hall at Holyrood to snatch her away. Perhaps Margaret's connection with the English court encouraged the fashion for black servants in England. Certainly they were, and remained, popular in Scotland. When the Scots King James VI also became James I of England, the fashion for entertainments on a black theme continued with Ben Jonson's elaborate 'Masque of Darkness' performed for Queen Anne of Denmark in 1605.[9]

The royal fascination with black people cast them very much in the role of curiosities but this was the age of discovery when daring sea-voyages brought increasing contact with the real black world. As early as 1533 Vice-Admiral Thomas Wyndham reached Benin and found that the king there spoke good Portuguese, having learnt the language as a child. He was also well aware of the niceties of European trading agreements, being quite happy to allow the English to have 80 tons of pepper, a valuable commodity, until their next voyage.[10] It would have been hard to see such a king as a mere exotic curiosity.

The Tudors were aware of the existence of a Moorish civilisation and Elizabeth I had first-hand knowledge of it. In 1577 she established official relations with Barbary and even forged a secret treaty with them, to send cannon balls in exchange for saltpetre. But when Sebastian of Portugal lost to the Moors at the battle of Alcazar in 1578, Catholic Europe blamed Elizabeth for the defeat. This certainly did not deter her. In 1600 a Moorish ambassador, complete with a retinue of fifteen other Moors, paid a state visit to England. It was evidently a fairly low-key affair, as by the standards of the sixteenth century fifteen was not a large retinue. Equally the Moorish embassy does not seem to have been considered particularly important at court. A French embassy of eighty people had been easily accommodated at royal expense earlier that year, but, according to Richard Hakluyt, court officials had great problems in finding both lodgings and hospitality for the Moors. They ended up spending seven months living alone in a house, with all sorts of rumours about their activities there floating about the court. Their curious habit of facing east when they slaughtered an animal was much talked about. Certainly they seem to have aroused a great deal of suspicion, with Hakluyt describing them as hateful and uncharitable, selling their leftover food to the poor rather than giving it away, as was expected of great households. What they made of the English is unknown.[11]

Given that there was some knowledge of black civilisation you might imagine that the Elizabethans developed respect for black people. Unfortunately this was not the case. There was an enormous appetite for books about all foreign countries, especially the more remote or newly discovered ones. Some of the reason for the interest was purely practical, as merchants required information to help them trade with such countries. Other people just wanted to hear stories, the more fantastical the better. The whole situation was complicated by the fact that although knowledge of Africa was increasing, it was still fairly basic and in some areas virtually non-existent. This led to the publication of books full of a strange mixture of information, some fact and some fiction. It was hardly surprising that the English developed some very odd ideas.

One book that was very fashionable at the time was called *The Fardle of Facions*, published in 1555. It was, in fact, a translation of a work written by Joannes Boemus and it owed a great deal to the ancient Greek historian Herodotus, who wrote in the fourth century BC. It certainly provided plenty of stimulation for those with a lively imagination. It confidently gives information not only on lions and rhinoceroses but also on dragons, which apparently preyed on elephants 'and sucke them to death, for their bloude'. Another myth it perpetuates is that of the fabulously wealthy kingdom of Ethiopia, where there was so much gold that even the prisoners' fetters were made from it. It was ruled not by a black king but by a white one, named Prester John.

Other books told of the strange peoples who lived in Africa, like the Syrbote, who stood 8ft high and lived by hunting elephants. The Ptoemphane were said to be governed by a dog, while the Arimaspi had only one eye, in the middle of their foreheads. No wonder there were those who chose to see black people as a link to a fairy-tale world.[12] But not all travel books were so fanciful. There were some, like Richard Hakluyt's *Principall Navigations*, which aimed to give as realistic a view as possible of the new countries being visited and the habits of the natives. Hakluyt's aims were really two-fold. He wanted to encourage English merchants to venture abroad not only for the glory of their country but also for commercial gain. His books include information on supposed voyages made by important historical figures, such as King Arthur's 'voyage to Island and the most Northeastern parts of Europe', confidently dated to the year

517. The idea was to suggest that England had a long history of epic voyages, which they were almost duty-bound to continue. Hakluyt's second aim was to provide factual information on navigation and the habits of the native peoples that would actually help modern adventurers. Fortunately his more up-to-date information was far more reliable, being based on first-hand accounts gleaned from people who had been on recent voyages. But even these were not designed to convince the English of the merits of the civilisations they encountered. Mr Thomas Sander's account of the voyage made to 'Tripolis in Barbarie' in 1583 is a thrilling account of how he was made a slave by the Turks, but managed to escape. It isn't altogether flattering to the Turks, but perhaps it helped a few people evade slavery.

Overall there was a mixed reaction to black people, and their experiences of living and working in England must have been as varied as those of white servants. Those working in the privileged world of the court or a fashionable household lived totally different lives from those who ended up in poor areas of London. However, whether they were seen as exotic fashion accessories for the rich or simply as servants, they were not considered as equal to white people, and the tempting profits to be made from the slave trade hardly encouraged a different approach.

THREE

Housewives, Husbandmen and Ploughmen Domestic and Farm Servants

The servants we shall look at in this chapter were very much those who did ordinary jobs for ordinary people. They didn't have the prestige that went with working in a great household or the excitement of preparing for the visits of the great and the good, but that is not to say that they were unskilled drudges whose lives were one long round of misery. Housewifery and farming manuals of the time indicate that the most able servants in this field had a wide range of skills and so enjoyed more variety of work than might be imagined. Equally, as they very much shared their employers' lives, many lived relatively comfortable lives, by the standards of the time.

Service at this level was divided into two discrete groups. On the one hand there were the people who lived in their employer's house, whom we shall refer to as servants, and on the other there were the day labourers, who lived in their own houses and usually worked on a seasonal rather than a regular basis. The servants who lived in were unmarried and usually young, while those who lived out tended to be married.[1]

First, we shall consider who these people were and who their employers were. Tudor society did not break down neatly into working, middle and upper classes. To modern eyes most Tudor people would be considered farmers, classed in the terms of the day as either husbandmen or yeomen. Even at the time there were no hard and fast definitions of either group, so your status tended to be decided not only by your own estimation of yourself but also by what your local community thought of you. Generally the husbandmen were the type of farmers often referred to in other times as peasants, who farmed small amounts of land usually with only the help of their family. The yeomen were better off, employing one or even several servants. The wealthiest yeomen could be very wealthy indeed. In 1524 Thomas Bradgate of Peatling Parva in Leicestershire was the richest yeoman in his county; astonishingly he also had the second highest tax assessment of anyone in the country, in any class.[2] Men like Bradgate could have lived the life of a gentleman, had they chosen to spend their money on fine clothes and other gentlemanly accoutrements. Instead, they preferred the simple life and remained yeomen despite their wealth. As you would expect, many of the husbandmen's children became servants. What is more surprising to us is that many of the yeomen's children did exactly the same.

As we have already seen, there was no stigma attached to being a servant in the sixteenth century. As it was in no way demeaning to have children in service, it was considered a useful way of training your children for their future life, as well as a way for them to save up for their future. The work they would be doing, either on the farm or in the house, was exactly the sort of work they would do after they were married and running their own house. Since they lived with their employer, they had neither the expense nor the responsibility of looking after themselves. In many ways it was an ideal bridge between childhood and adult responsibility.

It was also an excellent way to save for the future, provided you were self-disciplined. Servants' wages were not paid weekly but quarterly (or even annually), although servants could request payments during the year to buy necessities, with the balance being paid at the end of the year. There really wasn't a great deal you needed to buy for yourself, apart from some clothes. If you could resist the temptation to dress well it was an excellent opportunity to save money. This was particularly true for the men, and not only because they earned more than the women. Men were also often allowed to pasture sheep alongside their master's, like the eighteen-year-old from Essex who was hired in 1574/5 for 20*s* and the pasture for two sheep. This allowed servants to build up their own small flocks, which could either be transferred to their own farms when they married, or be sold to raise cash.[3]

The amount any servant could hope to earn varied enormously from area to area. For centuries the government had tried to keep wages down by legislation, the first attempts being triggered by the crisis brought about by the Black Death in the mid-fourteenth century. Most of the legislation had tried to keep wage levels down to specific given rates, but by the time the Statute of Artificers was passed in 1562 the authorities had realised that this was too inflexible. After this time the Justices of the Peace were ordered to meet annually and set wages for their county. This was done at one of the Quarter Sessions, when all the Justices of the county came together with all the other county officials – such as the coroners, high and petty constables – to sort out a wide range of civil administrative tasks. The records that survive for the Quarter Sessions from 1563 to 1566 show considerable variation. We also don't know if the set rates were adhered to, as there is so little evidence. What is certainly true is that women received only a fraction of men's wages.[4] Some servants were not paid at all, but received only their maintenance. The minimum ages for which rates are specified in the Quarter Session assessments vary from ten to twenty for men and from twelve to sixteen for women.

In terms of actual money received there are few records, but an agricultural labourer in the 1560s was paid around 3*s* 4*d* a week. This was not a great deal of money, considering that it cost about 5*s* to buy fodder for a horse for a week at this time.[5] Fortunately wages had been increasing since the mid-fifteenth century and continued to do so throughout the sixteenth century. In the period 1450–1650 the daily wage rates of agricultural labourers and building craftsmen in southern England increased from 4*d* to 1*s* and from 6*d* to 1*s* 5*d* respectively. The only problem was that the actual buying power of wages fell.[6] This would not have greatly affected the daily lives of the servants who lived in their master's house but of course it was a serious problem for the labourers who did not.

In terms of living conditions, domestic servants very much shared those of their masters. Inventories of houses do not talk of servants' rooms, simply because the servants slept wherever there was room for them. There was no feeling that somehow servants were inferior, and should be kept away from the family of the house to make a point. To understand how these servants could expect to live, it is therefore necessary to look at the houses and lifestyle of their masters. One of the important points about yeomen's houses is that they varied enormously throughout England. This point comes up again and again when you look at social conditions in the sixteenth century. There are, of course, still important regional differences today but they were even more marked at this time. Whether an area was primarily arable or pastoral also made a difference. All of this makes generalisation difficult, but it is possible to build up a picture of the kind of houses yeomen lived in.[7]

Yeomen living in Kent and parts of Surrey and Sussex tended to be the best off, as they lived on rich, productive soil. Their houses usually consisted of a hall with a two-storey wing built either side of it. By the end of the sixteenth century in most cases a floor had been installed in the hall to make the house two storeys throughout, and a brick fireplace and chimney had replaced the open fire that had once heated the hall. Cooking was usually done at this fireplace, as separate kitchens in this sort of house were unusual. After 1600 this changed, as more and more wives wanted both the convenience of a separate kitchen and the chance to move all the cooking equipment out of what was once the hall. Window glass was often installed. William Harrison in his *Description of England* published in 1577 commented that 'glass is come to be so plentiful and within a very little so good cheap'.[8] In fact, it was still quite a luxury but it was within the reach of the well-to-do, rather than only the rich. In the same way a yeoman with fashionable tastes, who perhaps had aspirations to become a gentleman, might install a framed timber staircase.

Some of these houses would have been very comfortable indeed by the standards of their day. John Browne of Raydon, Suffolk, despite being described as a husbandman, had a house with eight rooms plus a stable and a barn. The two ground-floor back chambers were both bedrooms. At the other end of the building was a buttery, used for the storage of beer, a backhouse (a general room used for cooking, brewing, baking, etc.) and even a kitchen. Rooms over the hall and buttery were used for storage. In many eyes John Browne must have been a yeoman rather than a husbandman.[9]

In County Durham, a much poorer area, a servant could expect a far more humble house to live and work in. The conditions here were comparable to those in Kent and Suffolk a century earlier. John Carter of Shincliffe, described as a yeoman, had goods worth a respectable £128 when he died in 1598, but only two or three rooms to live in. Ralph Billingham, who lived at the impressive-sounding Crook Hall, Brancepeth, had a hall, a parlour and a high chamber with two service rooms, a buttery and a milkhouse.[10]

In Devonshire, the Lake District and parts of Hertfordshire traditional byre houses were still being built into the seventeenth century. In such buildings the animals lived at one end in the byre and the people lived at the other end.

We are fortunate in having a plan of a theoretical ideal yeoman's house. Gervase Markham, in his *The English Husbandman*, first published in 1613, gives the layout of a house he considers suitable for 'a plain country man' (see plate 1 of the black and white plates). It is built on an 'H' plan, and was intended to be constructed from whatever materials were suitable to the area and the pocket of the owner, whether stud and plaster or stone. He intended that it be plain, but pointed out that you could add bay windows, battlements or perhaps a gatehouse if the owner had his eye on gentlemanly, rather than yeoman, status. The house is built in traditional style around a hall (A on the plan) with the service rooms on the left and the living rooms on the right. The service rooms consist of the dairy (L), milkhouse (M), kitchen (K), buttery (I) and an 'inward cellar within the buttery, which may serve for a larder' (H). Among the living rooms on the right are a room intended for visitors (strangers) marked as D, the dining parlour for entertaining guests (B) and an 'inward closet within the parlour for the mistress's use' (C). There is also a second storey, with rooms over the parlour, and private rooms for the owner over the kitchen and buttery. Markham's house appears rather old-fashioned, in that the hall seems open to the roof, instead of having a room over it. He also envisages a range of stables and barns and a poultry house, etc.

This house reflects the life of the yeoman. On the one hand it is very much a practical, working farm, while on the other, there are rooms for polite socialising, like the dining room and visitor's lodgings. This was an important point. Even Thomas Tusser,[11] who is ever warning his readers of the dangers of spending too much money, recommended what he terms 'measurely feasting' with the neighbours as part of your social duty. 'A lavish prodigality is brutish, so miserable covetousness is hellish', Markham reminds his housewife. This was a man who relied on farming for his living, but who had money enough for a few social niceties. It would have been a comfortable, practical house to live in by the standards of the day.

However, the rather pleasant house that Markham imagines his readers living in does not stop him, or other writers, from giving constant advice on thrift. The late sixteenth and early seventeenth centuries saw the rise of Puritanism, so this advice does have to be taken in the context of its time. Nevertheless you cannot get away from the fact that these were people to whom economy was necessary. Expensive, fashionable clothes (a great temptation to the Tudors) and lavish living would soon ruin them, for all they were not living in poverty. Markham reminds the housewife that she must be 'altogether without toyish garnishes, or the gloss of light colours, and as far from the vanity of new and fantastic fashions, as near to the comely imitations of modest matrons'.[12] Life at this level could be reasonably comfortable, but it was hardly luxurious. One of the marks of a yeoman, according to William Harrison's *Description of England*, was that he kept 'not idle servants, as gentleman do, but such as get both their own and part of their master's living'.[13] Servants of yeomen could expect reasonable food but plenty of hard work to go with it.

WOMEN'S WORK

John Fitzherbert, in his *Boke of Husbandrie* (1598), gave a summary of 'what labours a wife should doe in generall'. She was to start the day by giving thanks to God. After that, she had to sweep and tidy the house, milk the cows and feed the calves, then get the children up and ready for the day. She had to provide the family and any servants with breakfast, and, of course, dinner and supper later on. She had to send the corn to the miller to be ground, and perhaps malt too if necessary, being careful to measure both before they went in case the miller tried to cheat her. She also had to feed the poultry, make butter and cheese if it was the right time of year and feed the pigs. Again, at the right time of year she had to gather eggs from the poultry and keep an eye on sitting hens. As if this were not enough, she also had the garden to look after and flax, hemp and wool to process, plus buying and selling at the market.

No doubt this is an idealised version of the housewife's round, but it gives a feeling for the huge amount of work that needed to be done. From John Fitzherbert's list, it is easy to imagine that the women were doing all the work, but this wasn't the case. As we shall see later, the men were doing just as much, except their work was usually outdoors while the women were based within the house. Most work was divided into that deemed suitable for men, and that for women. We will have a closer look at the round of the housewife as described by Fitzherbert to understand the sort of work that a female domestic servant would be doing. It is impossible to cover all the work here. There was enough information written down at the time to fill several books, and doubtless there were many tricks of the housewife's trade that were never written down. The information given here will be enough to provide a flavour of the many skills women needed to possess and the sheer amount of hard work they had to do, as the female servants were expected to work alongside their mistress.

The housewife is told to start her day by giving thanks to God. Naturally, each individual housewife's personal attitude to devotion would have varied, but it was a serious issue. For one thing, the housewife was considered responsible for the moral upbringing of her children. Some thinkers of the day, such as Thomas Becan, who published a book called *The Catechism* in 1559, even advocated educating women purely because only a mother who could read could teach her children from the Bible. The other point was that disaster was never far away. Poor harvests, outbreaks of disease among livestock and, worse still, illness among the family were far more common than today. It was no wonder that the prudent housewife started her day with a prayer.

The day started early by our standards. Thomas Tusser recommends that all servants, male and female, should get up at four in the summer and five in the winter. Judging by the amount of work to be done, the master and mistress must have got up at the same time. The first task was sweeping and tidying, which was not necessarily as straightforward as it might seem, although the tidying at least might well have been easier than today. Manufactured goods were far more expensive in real terms in the sixteenth century than they are today, so there would have been fewer things lying around and waiting to be put away. In contrast, the sweeping might take a while. A wealthy yeoman might well have had stone or wooden floors on the ground floor, but beaten earth floors were still found in plenty of houses. Earth floors raised plenty of dust, and there must have been constant traffic across them. For example, any water needed for cleaning had to be carried in from the pump or well, so servants must have spent a great deal of time carrying heavy buckets of water around.

The dairy was always the concern of the mistress of the house, which was why the job of milking the cows was given to women. 'Man cow provides, Wife dairy guides' was how Thomas Tusser put it. Gervase Markham in his *English Housewife* suggests that the morning milking in spring and summer should be done between five and six. Considering that the housewife had already tidied and swept the house before doing the milking, she might well have been up before the servants. Running a good dairy was vital to the economy of the house. Cheese in particular contains large amounts of protein, and at a time when most people had hard, physical jobs its fat content was not a problem but a blessing. Butter was considered a food, to be eaten with a spoon, and not just something to spread on bread. The produce of the dairy was vital in keeping the family going. As Thomas Tusser advised:

> Where fish is scant, and fruit of trees
> Supplie the want with butter and cheese . . .

Excess cheese and butter could also be easily sold at the local market. However, the work involved in preparing dairy products was considerable. Everything had to be spotlessly clean or some of the processes would not work, or the butter or cheese could be tainted. As Markham put it, the dairy had to be so clean 'that a prince's bedchamber must not exceed it'.[14] He instructs that all the vessels used in the dairy had to be scalded once a day and dried in the open air.

The hard physical work involved in churning butter should not be underestimated either, and it had to be done at the right temperature. In the summer the churn was positioned in the coolest part of the dairy, perhaps in a bucket of cold water. In the winter the cold could stop the butter coming at all, so Markham suggests putting the cream in the churn while it is still hot from scalding, and also working near a fire. When the butter had been churned you still had to work it with your hands to extract the buttermilk, and salt it before it was finished. If you were potting up the butter for storage there was yet more work on top of that. Fortunately it seems that most housewives did not have so much milk to deal with that this job had to be done every day. In fact, Markham suggests that most housewives only made butter twice a week, on the days before the local market.

There were no shortcuts for the Tudor cheese-maker either. Today it is possible to use artificial rennet, but at this time rennet was made from the stomach of a suckling calf that had only ever had milk. It had to go through a series of processes before it was ready for use, including careful cleaning, washing and salting. Finally it was sealed up in a pot for storage. Markham recommends keeping the rennet for at least a year before using it. There is not the space here to go into the finer details of Tudor cheese-making, but it involved plenty of work.[15] Doubtless the knowledge that getting it wrong could ruin a whole batch of much-needed milk was enough to keep the housewife, or her servant, scrubbing, scalding and washing to keep the dairy spotless. Thomas Tusser in his *Hundredeth Pointes of Husbandrie* warned the housewife what would happen if she neglected her dairy:

> But huswives, that learne not to make their owne cheese
> With trusting of other, have this for their feese
> Their milke slapt in corners, their creame also lost:
> Their milk panners so slutie that their cheeses be lost.

The next major area of responsibility was cooking. In his list of the housewife's duties Fitzherbert cheerfully dismisses a day's cooking in one sentence, as if such work was just taken for granted. It may well have been, but the huge amount of work involved in preparing meals must have taken up a large part of the day. Cooking was still done over an open fire, which obviously had to be kept supplied with wood, which all had be chopped. Fortunately the mainstay of life at the time for most people was pottage, a sort of main course soup that contained just about anything. At the poorer end of society it could consist purely of vegetables, with some cereal to thicken it. At the richer end it comprised meat, usually pork, and sometimes appeared as one of the many dishes on the richest tables and included exotic imported ingredients such as almonds. Pottage was easy enough to produce, and once you had set it going it could be left to simmer, although obviously you had to keep an eye on the fire. This, together with bread, was the diet most servants could expect:

> Have millons at Michelmas, parsnips in Lent:
> In June buttered beans, saveth sith to be spent.
> With those and good pottage, inough having than
> Thou winneth the heart of thy labouring man.

The housewife didn't always get off so lightly. Thomas Tusser also reminds her that ploughmen expected roast meat as well on Thursdays and Sundays.

Thomas Tusser suggests that three dishes were quite enough for the table of a husbandman on most occasions, so there would be more than just pottage to prepare in many yeoman's houses. If the household was quite well-off, and particularly if it had pretensions to gentlemanly status, a great deal more would be on the table than pottage even on a daily basis. Both housewife and servant could end up having to produce far more complicated dishes when the family were entertaining. Housewifery books published in the late sixteenth and early seventeenth centuries are full of quite elaborate recipes, so it seems that the housewife and her servant had to be skilled cooks. The problem then was that you would be expected to produce a whole range of dishes at the same time, which would have put enormous strain not just on you and your servants, but also on the resources of your kitchen. For example, most kitchens would only have one fire and one spit, on which all the meat had to be cooked. Fortunately help was at hand in the form of some useful advice from Markham in his *English Housewife*.

The first thing the housewife had to work out was in what order to prepare the meat – which did not come conveniently oven-ready in those days. The animal had to be slaughtered, butchered, plucked, etc., before you even got to the stage at which Markham's instructions begin. He suggests breaking and crushing the bones of all joints of meat except a shoulder of mutton, and reminds you to cut off the feet of pigs or rabbits before you put them on the spit, and to take their heads off before they go to table. The pig also had to be cut in two, while capons, pheasants, chickens and turkeys had to be roasted with the pinions (end joints of the wing) folded up and the legs extended. He goes on to give instructions for quails, partridges, woodcock, snipes, bitterns and so on. Then, of course, came the problem of cooking joints of different sizes on a single spit over the fire. Keeping things hot was very difficult, so the only real answer was to have everything ready at the same time. Markham gives instructions for roasting a chine of beef, a loin of mutton, a lark and a capon at the same time, so that all are ready together. The instructions are quite complicated, involving not only the careful placing of everything on the spit but also a great deal of basting, and must have called for considerable skill.

Besides the general cooking there was also the baking of bread and brewing to consider, but these were not jobs that you would usually have to do every day. Heating up your bread oven was an expensive business so you would want to bake as infrequently as possible, although obviously this depended on the size of the household. The effort involved in kneading large amounts of dough is another reminder of the physical work women did. Markham even suggests doing some of this work by treading, rather than kneading.

It wasn't just the kneading that made work, either. The flour often had to be bolted through a cloth before baking could start. To make manchet, you had to use flour that had been finely ground, and also use a fine cloth for the bolting. Manchet was white bread, very much the luxury bread of its day. Ordinary domestic servants would not expect to eat it, but in wealthier yeomen households where the master hoped to be seen as a gentleman, the master and mistress and important guests might enjoy it. The flour for the finest grade of cheat bread, which was the next grade down from manchet, also required bolting but through a coarser cloth. In houses with fewer social pretensions bread was made with unbolted flour, often using a mixture of different flours such as barley or rye. This was the sort of bread that many servants would have eaten. Markham even suggests giving your servants the worst quality brown bread, which was made from a mixture of barley flour, wheat or rye flour, malt and ground pease. This flour was put through a meal sieve, but it certainly wasn't fine quality. He even suggests making the yeast mixture used for raising it as hot as possible, so that 'the less will the smell or rankness of the pease be received'.

However, the work of baking bread, for all it was a frequent task, paled into insignificance beside the work involved in brewing. Fortunately Fitzherbert, writing in the late sixteenth century, is rather old-fashioned in thinking that women had to brew every day. In the early sixteenth century brewing had been a frequent task, but in the middle of the century hops began to be introduced. These not only gave a distinctive flavour to beer, but also acted as a preservative. Before their introduction beer (then usually known as ale) went off very quickly, particularly in summer. The housewife had no choice but to brew little and often. Hops enabled her to brew much larger quantities far less often. Markham comments that his wife only brewed once a month.

In a world in which most water was contaminated, beer was the usual drink for most people and was therefore a necessity rather than a luxury – hence the existence of brew houses in so many Tudor houses. There were different grades of beer, some very strong and others very weak, but they were all made in basically the same way. The process was fairly simple. Ground malt was put in a vat and boiling water added to it. The mixture was left to stand, and then the liquid was drained off. The malt could then be used again, and indeed was often used as many as three times, although the resulting beer would be weaker with every use. Hops were then added to the drained liquid, and it was brought to the boil. Next it was strained to remove the hops, then yeast was added and it was put into barrels. Like so many sixteenth-century household chores it is easy to describe, but not so easy to do. The difficulty of moving heavy liquids around could be overcome by having your brewing vessels at different levels, so that each drained into the next. Even so, at some stage the water would have to be fetched from the pump in buckets to fill the lead, and a constant check had to be kept on each process.

We haven't, of course, yet come to the work involved in looking after the poultry or the garden, or in processing wool, hemp and flax into cloth. The children have only had a brief mention, yet of course they had to be looked after, and without modern benefits like washing machines or disposable nappies. It is at this stage also important to point out that in fact most Tudor housewives did not make everything their families wore. They might possibly make a pair of sheets or a few blankets, but most people bought their clothes, new or second hand, or the cloth to make them. Likewise, while both Markham and Fitzherbert expected a woman to make malt for brewing, it was quite possible to buy it. Even so, the sheer amount of work that a yeoman's wife and her female servants had to get through is obvious. The range of skills that both were required to have is also impressive, considering we haven't even touched on areas such as preserving or making medicines. Working as a domestic servant must indeed have been a good opportunity for a young girl to learn how to run her own house.

MEN'S WORK

Books on husbandry show that Tudor men were not exactly sitting around chatting while their women worked. In another of Gervase Markham's books, *Markham's Farewell to Husbandry*, he gives an overview of a typical day for a ploughman in January, which was considered the start of the agricultural year. He was to get up before four in the morning and, like the housewife, start his day with prayers. He then had to go to the stables and feed his plough-horses or team of oxen (or indeed both), and muck out their stalls. After that he had to groom them, water them and feed them again. While they were eating he prepared the harness. Markham reckoned that all this would take two hours, and so by six the ploughman was ready to go in to breakfast, for which he would be allowed half an hour. Next he harnessed the animals, and by seven he would be out ploughing. He would expect to work at that until two or three in the afternoon, then he would bring the plough team home, groom them and feed them, and then go to his own dinner about four o'clock. Again he was allowed half an hour for his meal, after which he would groom the team, muck out, give them more food and then go to the barns to prepare their fodder for the next day. He would then water the animals again and feed them again, by which time it would be past six o'clock. At this time he would eat his supper, but even after that he was not free to do as he liked. Instead Markham suggests that he mends shoes, either for himself or other members of the household, beat and knock hemp or flax, stamp apples for cider, grind malt, peel rushes for making rush lights (the standard cheap form of lighting at the time) or do some similar job until eight o'clock. He then had to go out to the stable again, muck out and litter the animals down for the night and finally feed them again. Only after that could he go to bed, by which time he must have been exhausted.

The amount of work a ploughman did was partly due to the number of draught animals needed. Naturally this varied according to the soil, but Markham reckons either four, six or eight animals for the plough, four or five for pulling a cart and at least six for the big hay wains. All these animals had to be groomed, fed and watered all year round.

There was also a great deal more ploughing to be done in the sixteenth century than today. Modern farmers usually plough just once, in the autumn, but in Tudor times fallow arable land was typically ploughed three times a year if it was to be used for wheat the next year, and sometimes even four times. The ploughing was done so that the weeds growing on it would be ploughed back in to add nutrients to the soil. It was given a shallow ploughing in April once the crops had been sown in the other fields. In June it was ploughed deeper, and then it was ploughed again in July or August. It was then harrowed twice, and the clods of earth remaining were either rolled or beaten by hand with a mattock or with a clodding beetle, an implement that resembled a carpenter's mallet.[16]

The amount you could expect to plough in a day was also tiny compared with today. Of course, even today there are no hard and fast rules about how much you can plough per day. Obviously there are variables, such as the power of the tractor and the size of the plough, but 10 to 15 acres is a reasonable estimate. Markham thought ploughing an acre or an acre and a half per day was reasonable in heavy soil, but even in light soil 2 or 3 acres was as much as one team could manage.

Agriculture has never been an option for shirkers, but the sheer amount of work involved in farming before the introduction of machinery is quite incredible. It was no wonder that master and servant alike worked long hours. When it came to the harvest, for example, Markham thought a man might mow an acre of hay in a rough meadow per day or an acre and a half in a good meadow. When it came to cutting oats or barley, an acre and a half per man was reasonable for a good, thick crop, but if the crop was poor and thin a man might cut up to 4 acres.

Another example of the extra work there was to do at this time centred around the old gardener's favourite, fertiliser. Getting enough fertiliser was a constant problem. Certainly the farmer's own animals didn't produce enough manure to do the job alone. Farmers therefore had to use whatever was available in their locality. In Newcastle upon Tyne the townspeople put their ashes and dung on a heap next to the castle walls in the middle of the town (which must have made the place smell more interesting than most!) so that once a year the farmers could come in and take it away. Some of it was even carried by sea to coastal areas. In some areas marl was dug from marlpits, while in others limestone could be carried for 2 to 4 miles to be burnt in kilns, before it was put on the fields. Around Padstow in Cornwall people collected sea sand, loaded it onto horses and travelled as far as 6 miles to put it on the fields. In Hertfordshire farmers laid bracken on the lanes in the autumn, left it over the winter to get well trodden, and then put it on the fields. London's stable dung was carried by river to Chelsea, Fulham, Battersea and Putney. Malt dust left by maltsters, soap ashes thrown out by soap boilers, brine from the Cheshire salt pits, decaying fish entrails and offal were all used. There was also, of course, the contents of the privy which could be put to good use. Tusser puts this job down as one to be done in November:

Foule privies are now to be cleansed and fide
Let night be appointed such baggage to hide:
Which buried in garden, in trenches alowe
Shall make very many things better to growe.

And no matter how unpleasant it was to handle, it was the farmer and his men who had to spread it on the fields by hand.

The yeoman farmer and any male servants had to have as wide a range of skills as the housewife. There was not only the ploughing and the plough team to look after. The exact work required in each area obviously depended on the soil, and whether the area was largely pastoral or arable. A man could find himself dealing with sheep, pigs, cows, oxen and horses, and he had to know how to deal with their illnesses. Any animals kept for meat for home use he also had to slaughter and butcher. He also kept bees. He had to know about growing a variety of crops, from cereals to fruit. He had to dig ditches and lay hedges, and maintain them, not to mention making and repairing a wide range of farm implements: 'if every young husband(man) shall with his penny buy all these things, he shall finde the cost great and unsavoury, wherefore it shall be necessary for him to learne, and practice [*sic*] to make his yoakes, ore-bowles, stooles and all manner of plough implements, with his owne laborious hands,' warned John Fitzherbert.

Tusser, too, suggests similar work for the men:

Thy servant, in malking, thy pastures aboute:
For yokes, forkes and rakes let him loke to fine oute
And after at leyser, let this be his nier:
Trim them and make them, at home by the fier.

On top of this was the huge amount of work involved in bringing home the harvest. The young farm servant had a lot to learn before he was ready to set up in farming himself.

One thing that is very much apparent from the lives of yeomen and their servants is that teamwork was crucial. Thomas Tusser made the point that if husband and wife fell out and stopped cooperating, the effects were dire:

> Housekeping and husbandry, if it be good
> Must love one another, as cousinnes in blood
> Thy wife to, must husband as well as the man
> Or farewell thy husbandry, doe what thou can.

In the same way it was vital to choose the right servants, as idle or untrustworthy ones were more trouble than they were worth:

> Beware raskabilia, slough full to wurke
> Prolointers and filchers, that love for to lurke . . .

Finding servants, or finding employment as a servant, must have been done to a great extent by word of mouth. When employer and servant agreed on terms, the contract they made was purely verbal, but the fact that it had been made was usually recorded in some place, such as the records of the Quarter Sessions or the Petty Sessions. (The Petty Sessions took place when two or three Justices of the Peace came together to deal with a range of issues, such as trying and convicting minor offences and ordering reputed fathers to maintain their bastard children. These meetings were much smaller and less formal than the Quarter Sessions.) The master would present the servant with some kind of payment, known as the 'earnest', 'hiring penny', 'fastening penny' or 'God's penny' to seal the bargain. The Justices of the Peace sometimes fixed this amount. In Essex in 1612 it was limited to 1*d*.[17]

Michaelmas (29 September) was the usual time for hiring in the south and east, and Martinmas (11 November) in the north. This was a convenient time as the harvest had finished and there was a lull in agricultural activity. In the sixteenth century the usual thing was for masters and servants to meet just before the sessions. They would make agreements that would then be formalised at the sessions. The great hiring fairs developed from this process, but not until the eighteenth century.

The idea of hiring purely at this one time of year was so fixed that if for some reason a contract started later than the usual date, it ran only until the next hiring season. There were two main reasons for this. The first was that it was convenient for masters and servants to be seeking each other out at the same time, and the second was the Elizabethan fear of vagrants. The authorities didn't like people on the road without good reason. Hiring was seen as a good reason, but the authorities were less nervous if it all happened at a particular time of year.

The contracts bound the servant to serve the master and obey his reasonable commands, while the master was to maintain the servant for the year and pay the wages as agreed, whether or not there was work for the servant, and whether or not the servant was fit to work. Not all masters seem to have been willing to do this. The Hertfordshire records show that a certain Anthony Gray had to be ordered to keep and maintain his servant Jeffrey Salmon who had become subject to 'strange fits of lunacy' until the end of his agreed term of service.[18] Equally, female servants who fell pregnant could find themselves thrown out, even if the father of their child was the master of the house or one of the family.

Due to the lack of records, it is difficult to know to what extent servants were exploited. The problem is, as ever, that the records do not mention the good employers, only those who were bad. Certainly there were terrible cases of exploitation which came before the courts and of course there must have been others which never came out into the open. In 1574 in Essex there was a case of a master who not only raped his female servant but also forced her to take an oath to conceal what had happened. To make things even worse, he had also retained her wages.[19]

There was also the strange case of Joan Reyner, who unfortunately got caught up in a marital dispute between her employer, the parson of Alphamstone in Essex, and his wife. There were only three beds in the house, one of which was used by the parson and his wife, another by Symond Callye, the parson's wife's son from a previous marriage, and the third, which Joan slept in. The parson and his wife had an argument, after which they refused to sleep together for two weeks. This forced Joan to sleep with Symond and, according to the record 'not having the feare of God before her eyes, being overcome with the entyceing and allurement of the same young man, consenting to his wicked demand, is now become with child . . .'. How much choice Joan actually had in the matter is not known, but, to add insult to injury, the parson seems to have wanted to throw Joan out. He had to be ordered to keep her for the rest of the year.[20]

People often imagine that servants stayed working for the same employer for years, but this was the exception rather than the rule. As Thomas Tusser remarked: 'The stone that is rolling can gather no mosse/for maister and servant, oft changing is losse.' Perhaps this was mere wishful thinking on his part, because contracts usually only lasted for a year and many servants chose to move on after this time. Some must have moved for the sake of change but others may have moved to widen their experience. Perhaps they felt that if they stayed in one place for too long they would get taken for granted. The relationship between master and servant cannot always have been easy to manage.

RELATIONS BETWEEN MASTERS AND SERVANTS

The master of the house was seen as responsible for his servants' behaviour and moral upbringing, just as he was for his own children. The reason for this was perfectly reasonable. As we have seen, most of the servants were very young and must have needed someone to take the place of their parents in supervising their behaviour. The authorities understood and made use of this situation. In 1540, when the government was particularly anxious about the state of foreign relations and was thinking of its preparations for war, an edict declared that masters had to supply not only their sons but also their servants aged between seven and seventeen with a bow and arrows. The only important difference from the servant's point of view was that the master paid for his children's equipment, but was allowed to deduct the cost of the servant's from his wages.[21]

It is possible to get a feeling of how masters and their servants rubbed along together. Many of the books on housewifery and husbandry produced at this time gave hints on how to manage servants. These books were, of course, written by employers rather than employees and they do describe the ideal situation, but at least they give an idea of how the whole master and servant relationship was supposed to work at this level.

Thomas Tusser's *Five Hundred Points of Good Husbandry* stresses that masters had obligations to their servants, and not just servants to masters. It was the master's duty to treat his servants fairly by paying them on time. The labourers were to be paid weekly and the servants quarterly. On the other hand it was a mistake to reward servants too well, as then you ran the risk of going without yourself. When it came to food, the same idea applied. Servants were to be well, but not over, fed. 'Poor seggons [labourers] halfe staved work faintly and dull/And lubbers doo loiter, their bellies too full,' Tusser reminded his readers. He even suggests that breakfast should only be given to those who deserve it, and that servants were to be sent out to work without being told what was for dinner. They were supposed to concentrate on their work, not their meals.

Then there was the matter of discipline. In a very hierarchical society it was only to be expected that servants were to be kept strictly in awe of their masters and mistresses. However, as servants and masters lived so closely together, too much shouting and violence was hardly in anyone's interests. 'Much brawling with servant, what man can abide?' as Tusser put it. In any case a good master and mistress would know how to keep the servants in order without fighting: 'A wand in thy hand/though ye fight not at all/makes youth to their business better to fall.' Good servants also had a right to be shown friendship by their employers, and to expect praise when they did a job well. 'Use labourers gently, keepe this as a law' was Tusser's recommendation.

This advice was particularly important at harvest time. If you paid your labourers fully and on time, gave them the gifts they expected (it was traditional for the reapers to be given gloves, for example) and treated them to a good harvest home supper, then there was a good chance that they would come back to work for you next year. As labour was always short at harvesting, it was wise to keep your labourers on your side.

In the same spirit it was the employer's duty to look after his servants when they were ill. Heresbach in his *Foure Bookes of Husbandry*, published in London in 1577, points out that servants will be more faithful and work better when they are well if they have 'good cherishing in their sicknesse'. Tusser also pointed out that a sick servant should not be looked after grudgingly, as 'a thing of a trifle shall comfort him much'. We can only hope that masters who turned out sick servants, as we have seen above, were rare.

Masters and servants relied on one another. There was simply so much work to be done that a husbandman was most successful when the whole family, including the servants, pulled together. Tusser pointed out that a careless servant, a mistress who was forever scowling, a 'giddy brain' master and a hog that eats the poultry were all a threat to the husbandman's survival. The master and mistress, no less than the servants, had to work hard and exercise restraint if the farm was to prosper.

During the sixteenth century increasing numbers of yeomen found themselves dealing not only with servants but also with tenants. After the dissolution of the monasteries large amounts of land came onto the market, which meant that from the late 1530s yeomen had an increasing chance of owning enough land to become landlords. Needless to say, there was plenty of advice available for the new landlord on how to treat tenants. Robert Furse of Morshead, who was himself a yeoman landlord, had this to say to his children in 1593 regarding tenants: 'Burden them not with more fines, rents or services than they be well able to pay you, displace not an honest, friendly tenant for a trifle or small sum of money.'[22]

It was always tempting for a landlord to put up the rent. Thomas More complained in his famous book *Utopia* of gentlemen whose tenants 'they poll and shave to the quick by raising their rents' in order to finance their lavish lifestyles. Thomas Tusser too pointed out that a good landlord was blessed by God, while a bad landlord was a 'husbandman's rod'. Of course, it was really in the interests of both landlord and tenant that rents be kept reasonable, thus allowing the tenant to run the farm well. Good relations between landlord and tenant relied on give and take, just as did relations between masters and servants.

Whatever their relationship with their master, most servants gave up full-time service around the age of twenty-five. In bad economic times the age of leaving service tended to go up, only to fall again as things improved. This was because most left in order to marry. As you could only marry when you had enough money to set up your own household, the harder the times, the longer couples had to wait.[23]

Leaving the relatively safe world of service and setting up on your own was a very big step indeed. You now had to find your own food and lodging, not to mention being able to provide for any children that might come along. Many small-scale farmers found that in order to make ends meet they needed to work for wages at least part of the year, but the life of the labourer was very different from the life of the servant.

LABOURERS

Labourers were casual workers, paid by the day or even by the area of land they had to work. The farmer's live-in servants usually did the prestigious work, particularly that involving handling horses, while the labourers would often be employed for strenuous work such as hedging, digging ditches or helping to bring in the harvest. Women and children often gathered stones, weeded, cut rushes, trod hay or picked apples. Labourers were also expected to provide their own tools, while farm servants used those provided by the farmer.

Labourers, just like yeomen, came from a variety of backgrounds. A landless labourer, living in some kind of hovel and making do with what work he could get, had a much harder life than a labourer who had his own smallholding and grazing rights on the local common. The houses they lived in showed the difference. The poorer labourers occupied unpleasant hovels but others lived in what were really quite attractive cottages. As usual, there were regional variations. Of those labourers' cottages that are recorded, in the Welsh Marches and north-west England most only had one room but in the East Riding of Yorkshire nearly a third had more rooms. Nearly two-thirds of labourers in the East Midlands had more than one room, while in Hertfordshire being so poor as to only have a single room was unusual – in fact, only one-tenth of cottages contained just a single room. Of those of which we have some description, most had a living room (usually called the hall) with a chamber at one end, or more usually above. There was often a buttery opening off the hall, and some larger cottages even had a milkhouse, dairy or cheese chamber. The cooking was usually done over the fire in the hall. About half the houses also had some kind of outhouse, such as a barn, stable or woodshed. Life for a labourer was certainly not luxurious but the better-off ones enjoyed more agreeable lives than we often expect. Like the yeomen, their living conditions gradually improved at the end of the sixteenth century and into the seventeenth, with their houses gradually becoming bigger.

It is difficult to know what conditions the very poorest labourers lived in as few people recorded anything about them. They were too poor to make wills, and had too few possessions for anybody to bother making any kind of inventory of their belongings when they died. Richard Carew in his *Survey of Cornwall*, published in 1602, describes older cottages as having low, thatched roofs, earth walls, few partitions, no floorboards or glass windows and a simple hole in the wall to let out the smoke, instead of a chimney.

Labourers made up a large percentage of the population. Given the lack of records it is impossible to know exactly how many there were but estimates suggest that they made up between a quarter and a third of the entire rural population.[24] Despite the gradual increase in size of the better-off labourers' houses, the end of the sixteenth century was not a good time for the poorer ones. As we have seen above, the real value of their wages was decreasing. To make matters worse, there was more and more pressure on land owing to the increasing size of the labour force as the population grew.

An act passed in 1589 ordered that no cottage should be built with less than 4 acres of land attached to it, which was presumably about the amount of land you needed in order to keep a family. The increasing size of the population made it harder and harder for the poorer labourer to have access to enough land to do this. Although it was usual among the middle and upper classes for a father to leave the bulk of his possessions to his eldest son, this was not the case in the lower classes, for whom it was much more usual for the property to be shared out among the sons. Although this helped the younger sons, it did mean that farms could get smaller and smaller until they were scarcely viable. The increasing population also made the size of the labour force bigger, but the amount of employment available did not increase with it. Manufacturing industry only employed about a fifth of the workforce by 1650 and there may even have been less agricultural work available as farms became larger and better organised. The Statute of Artificers and Poor Laws of the time also discouraged people from moving to look for work, which made things worse.[25]

Fortunately labourers often had other means of making a living besides farm work and cultivating any land they might have. Many were involved in the woollen industry, and carded or spun wool, knitted socks or sometimes even wove cloth. There were also some local industries that could provide work. In Dorset there was glove making, and in Cornwall the production of rush mats. There were also certain additions to farm wages that some labourers received, such as the right to pasture sheep on the farmer's land and gifts of items of clothing, like the gloves received at harvest time. For many of them, though, the time they spent working as servants before they married must have been the most prosperous period of their lives.

FOUR

Lords and Ladies, Bishops and Princes
Life in a Great Household

DAILY LIFE

Great households were usually very good places to live and work in the Tudor period. Far from being exploited, the servants, whether gently bred or not, were well treated and well rewarded. Even domestic servants, who frequently moved jobs when employed in lower-class houses, often stayed for years. For example, many of the surnames of servants found in the accounts of John Howard, 1st Duke of Norfolk, in 1462 are also to be found in those of the 2nd Duke in 1525.[1]

The employees of a great household came from a wide range of backgrounds. Domestic servants were often recruited from the lord's estates and usually came from peasant or yeoman families. There would also be a number of clerics employed to meet the household's spiritual needs. At one time clerics were also employed as administrators, but by the sixteenth century this work was usually done by lay people, sometimes even by professional lawyers. Often there were foreigners working in the household, especially in the case of families like that of Viscount Lisle, who was Henry VIII's Governor of Calais. Families with city connections often employed men of various classes and backgrounds from London. There would be the sons of the gentry and aristocracy who were either working or being educated, depending on their age, or even doing both at once. We should also take into account the mix of visitors who constantly came and went.

Perhaps the greatest surprise to the modern eye would be the almost complete lack of women. This was the case even when the leader of the household was a lady, rather than a man. Great households had been largely made up of men since the Middle Ages, dating back to the days when most of the household comprised the lord's army. It was also more expensive, and therefore more prestigious, to employ men than women, which was an important point when part of the aim in having a great household was to display your wealth. There was even a feeling of hostility to women in some households where it was felt that employing them led to trouble. If any members of the household were married, their wives usually lived elsewhere. Single men were always both more numerous and more likely to be promoted.[2] The only women usually employed at the domestic level in a great household were laundresses, and they often lived nearby, rather than in the household itself.

The only exceptions to the rule were the personal attendants of the lady of the house. In such a male-dominated environment the main job of these attendants was to provide companionship, and consequently they tended to be ladies rather than women, that is, they were close enough to the rank of the lady to be personal friends rather than mere servants. This was why ladies often employed more personal attendants than their husbands. Lady Margaret Long of Hengrave Hall employed about five maids for herself and her daughters between 1541 and 1564, plus two male servants of the chamber. [3]

A grand lady usually employed a few well-bred young girls among her ladies. It was part of her duty. Just as young gentlemen, if given the opportunity, would obtain social polish by attending a great lord, so young ladies achieved the same end by attending a great lady. Such young girls usually joined the household around the age of fourteen, having completed whatever formal education was considered suitable for them by their family. They would usually stay until a marriage was arranged for them.

The whole of a great household revolved entirely around the one lord or lady who owned it. Even other members of the family were very definitely of secondary importance. They simply were not part of the household often enough to be anything else. Wealthy sixteenth-century families did not see that much of one another. Even in the nursery children were not necessarily kept with their parents. If their parents went to court, for example, the children would definitely be left at home, as the court was considered no place for infants. Once they left the nursery, they were often sent into other noble houses to be educated, sharing tutors with other children of the aristocracy. Before the dissolution one alternative was to send girls to convents and boys to monasteries until the age of about fourteen. Bridget Plantagenet, daughter of Lord Lisle, was educated at St Mary's Convent in Winchester, while her stepbrother George Basset was sent to Reading Abbey.[4] After this time, if a place could be found for them, girls would be sent off into another household and boys were launched on various different paths, depending on their parents' aspirations for them. Girls sometimes returned home for a short time before their marriage, but in general wealthy Tudor children saw little of their parents.

In order to understand what it was like living in one of these households you need some idea of the daily routine. Life was obviously very different for the well-bred servants, who were not expected to do manual work, from that of domestic servants, but everyone had their place and was considered very much part of the household. In fact many of the activities of the household, such as dining, were done corporately with the deliberate intention of building up a sense of community. It is difficult to know some of the finer details of life in great households owing to lack of evidence. There are also bound to have been differences between households. They were, after all, private households whose rules and regulations reflected to some extent the opinions of the master or mistress of the house. Even so, enough pieces of the jigsaw survive to give us a general feel of what went on.

The day started early by our standards, and there was a summer and a winter timetable, partly to make best use of the natural light. Artificial lighting was expensive and even wax candles, the best artificial light available, were nowhere near as good as daylight. The Duke of Northumberland's cooks had to get up at four, and the head household officers at five. In the household of Prince Edward in 1473 the gates were officially opened at five in summer and six in winter, so this seems to have been a fairly normal time to be up and about.[5]

The first business of the day, at least for the upper household, was not breakfast but a church service. Religion played an enormous part in the life of the household, particularly before the Reformation. The 3rd Duke of Buckingham insisted that 'no good governaunce in politick rule may be had without service to God as well'.[6] He even insisted that all members of his household were to attend mass every day, although it is difficult to know whether the domestic servants did so in practice. Most of them must have been too busy with their duties. It would certainly not have occurred to most ordinary people at this time to attend mass daily, even if they had the time.

From the architectural viewpoint, great houses certainly had plenty of space to allow daily worship even in the largest household. There were usually several chapels. Castle Hedingham in Essex had at least four by 1513.[7] Portable altars could also be used to allow services to take place in rooms usually used for other things. The existence of so many chapels was quite deliberate as it was not the intention that the whole household should worship together. To preserve the household hierarchy, members of the household worshipped in different places according to their rank. The most prestigious place to be seen was the lord's small personal chapel, where only the most senior members of the household attended. After that there was a hierarchy of places, with the largest generally being the least prestigious.

For the upper members of the household, breakfast followed the religious service. Breakfast was not served automatically at this time, although it was becoming more common. The lord, his wife and children and the senior officers of the household could expect it, but not the rest of the staff. Where it was supplied, it was taken to people's private chambers rather than being served in public. The Earl of Northumberland had his breakfast served at eight o'clock, which was a long time after getting up by modern standards.

The next important landmark in the day was dinner, which at this time was served during the day, while supper was the evening meal. Dinner was served between nine and eleven in the morning, depending on the time of the year and the household. This seems early to us, but for those who had not eaten breakfast it was the first meal of the day. In any case it would hardly have seemed early to those who had been up since four or five.

By the sixteenth century, and particularly by the time of Elizabeth I, it was increasingly common for the lord to dine privately, but there were still occasions when he would dine in public. In either case, serving his dinner involved considerable ceremony (see the section on gentlemen servants for details). Even if the lord was dining privately his food would be processed through the hall, where it would be shown due honour. The 1609 Ordinances of Henry, Earl of Huntingdon, state that an usher was to 'cause all men in the hall to come to the other side of the hall and be bare-headed while their Honnor's meate passeth through'.[8]

Dinner could take up to two hours, especially if the lord was present, which is in stark contrast to the meagre half-hour allowed for farm hands, domestic servants in lower households and the like. Even if the lord was not present, the meal was still served with due ceremony. The lord's place would be taken either by his wife or, in the absence of the family, by a senior household officer such as the steward. However, the lower servants did not necessarily get a long break for lunch. In really grand households, such as the monarch's, there had to be two different sittings for dinner so that everyone could be fed. Even so, each sitting lasted an hour, which was a good break by Tudor standards.

During the afternoon the household would disperse to their various duties. Evensong was the next time when most of the household would probably come together. Again, we cannot be sure who exactly attended, or if the whole household was expected to be present. In any case, evensong was followed by supper. This was served between four and five, depending on the time of year, and was usually a less formal meal than dinner.

After supper it was generally time for relaxation, at least for those not involved in washing up. There might be entertainment of some kind. The day ended, at least for the upper servants, with a ceremony known as the 'all night', mentioned by John Russell,[9] in which the lord was formally put to bed. The gates of the house were closed between nine and ten. Overall, the hours of work in the household do not seem to have been unreasonable when you consider that Gervase Markham's husbandman (see p. 56) was expected to be up before four o'clock and seems to have gone to bed about nine.

The daily routine of the house was, of course, not unvarying. It changed not only with the seasons but also with the church year. Kitchen accounts show that the food served varied considerably according to the demands of the church, even on a weekly basis. In most households Friday was a fast day on which meat would not be served. Those households with a more devoted religious feel even observed fasts on Wednesdays and Saturdays. The church recommended these as fast days, but did not insist on their observance. On the other hand Sunday was always a day for feasting.

The annual feasts and fasts of the church were very much observed. Usually no meat was eaten throughout Lent, although contrary to popular belief most households continued to eat eggs. Ash Wednesday, Maundy Thursday and Good Friday were complete fast days. The good news was that the feast of the Annunciation, known as 'Lady Day' (25 March), often fell during Lent, which gave everyone a day off from fasting. Other feast days generally observed were the birthday of John the Baptist (29 June), the Assumption of the Virgin Mary (15 August) and Michaelmas (29 September). All Saints' Day and All Souls' Day (1 and 2 November) were also times when it was usual to hold requiem masses to remember the dead associated with the household.

The Christmas holiday brought the greatest changes to the life of the household. The staff had to start preparations in October and November as specialist supplies such as sugar and exotic imported fruit like dates had to be bought well in advance. Animals were bought at the same time, so they could be fattened. Advent was observed as a fast, with the celebrations and feasting only beginning on Christmas Day itself. Despite this, guests often started arriving from the Feast of the Immaculate Conception (8 December).

Besides the feasts and fasts that were observed generally, each household had a calendar of festivals all of its own. The feasts of the family's patron saints were often observed, for example. Twelve-month minds, held a year after a funeral, were other feasts that were very personal to individual households. Sometimes these were held not only for important people, like members of the lord's family, but for relatively humble servants. Elizabeth Stonor held one for her chamberer in 1469.[10] These more personal celebrations must have been particularly important in creating a sense of belonging in the household.

Despite this carefully nurtured sense of community, by the sixteenth century households spent at least part of the year broken up. Great lords were obliged to spend more and more time at court, and it simply wasn't practical to arrive there with your entire household. No royal palace was big enough to house all the great lords in attendance together with their entire staffs. The number of people you were allowed to bring to the palace was strictly limited, and all the rest had to be housed elsewhere at your own cost. If the court was at Whitehall, there was the possibility of using the lord's London house but even this would have become harder as the fashion grew for smaller but more fashionable London houses. The solution was for a small number of servants to accompany the lord to court and for the rest to be sent home on board wages until they were needed again.[11]

Despite the fact that households were frequently broken up, by the standards of the time a great household was a very secure place to work. As long as you were trustworthy and managed not to offend your employer, you could have a secure job for life. Many people did not live long enough to worry about old age, but often employers were generous to those who became too old to work. Pensions, annuities and lump sums were often left to individual servants in wills. This help was, of course, purely at the discretion of the employer but it was still far more than most people could hope for at the time. However, despite their relative security, there was one serious drawback in being a member of a great household. When the master or mistress died, their household was broken up for good, with no guarantees of employment by the heir.

The last duty of a member of a great household was to take part in the funeral of his lord or lady. In the sixteenth century the aristocracy staged huge funerals, involving enormous numbers of people. Some nine hundred people took part in the funeral of Edward Stanley, Earl of Derby, who died in 1572.[12] They were intended not only to demonstrate the importance of the deceased, but also to show that despite a death, order and stability were being maintained. It was for this reason that the lord's entire household, and not just the senior officers, took part. At Elizabeth I's funeral her entire household took part, from the highest officers to the lowest scullions.

The household would not be broken up immediately on the death of the lord. For one thing, it took several weeks to organise such an enormous event as an aristocratic funeral and the household was obviously needed to do the work. The Earl of Derby conveniently died at Latham House, just 2 miles from Ormskirk parish church, where he was to be buried, but it still took six weeks to organise his funeral. Sometimes it took much longer if a body had to be brought home from abroad. Sir Henry Unton happened to be on embassy in France when he died in 1596, so his body had to be brought home for burial.

The funeral procession of a great person was designed so that they went to their grave surrounded by ceremony, just as they had lived. It is worth giving a brief description of the very elaborate procession that accompanied the Earl of Derby's body, just to give a sense of the incredible pageantry involved.

The first part of the procession included a hundred poor men marching two by two, followed by forty men and boys of the choir, dressed in their surplices. The central part of the convoy was mounted, and started with eighty of the earl's gentlemen, followed by his two secretaries, fifty knights and esquires riding two abreast, the earl's two chaplains, and the three chief officers of his household, the steward, treasurer and comptroller, bearing their white staves of office. Next came a mounted esquire carrying the late earl's banner. This was followed by four elaborately dressed heralds bearing his heraldic achievements and carrying his parcel gilt (that is, particularly gilded) steel helmet and his sword. Directly behind them came the coffin itself, borne on a chariot draped with a large black velvet pall and drawn by four horses, each ridden by a page. The chariot itself was escorted by four hooded esquires on horseback, with six more outriders carrying bannerols.[13] Behind the chariot rode the chief mourner (in this case the earl's heir) and behind him rode the late earl's Gentleman of the Horse, leading the riderless horse of estate which was covered and trapped with black. After him came the more distinguished mourners, all relatives of the deceased, and finally two yeomen ushers who conducted no fewer than five hundred yeomen on foot, who formed the last section of the procession.

The idea was to show that the whole social unit that had surrounded the earl in life was still in place after his death. It was only when the coffin was placed in its final resting place that the chief officers of the household would ritually break their rods of office and throw them into the grave. This was the official acknowledgement that the old household no longer existed. In this case the new Earl of Derby was to retain his predecessor's chief officers, but they only officially received their new offices and their new rods of authority at the funeral banquet.

The Earl of Derby's officers were extremely lucky to be retained. It was by no means certain that the heir of a great man would want all, or perhaps any, of his predecessor's household. If the heir was an adult, he would already have his own household. When

Lord Burghley died, his son Robert was already a well-established figure in politics himself, and he did not need his father's servants, nor did he have his father's financial resources to employ them. It was for this reason that it was usual for a lord to bequeath his servants a number of months' wages, or sometimes even a number of years' wages. Six months' wages was quite common, but Burghley went as far as to leave his staff four years' wages.[14] In modern terms, they were receiving redundancy pay.

Despite the communal nature of life in a great household, experiences were very different for the upper and lower servants. The two groups came from varied social backgrounds and had diverse expectations, so we will now look at the lives of the two groups separately, starting with the domestic servants.

FIVE

Yeomen, Scullions and Children
Living in a Great Household as a Lower Servant

This chapter will look at the lives of those who worked in the less glamorous part of the household. These were the people who cooked, baked bread, made candles and chopped wood. They did not usually wear the elaborate liveries given to those who worked in more prestigious jobs, and were very much the 'backroom boys' who made possible the luxurious life enjoyed by the lord and many other members of the household. But even though they were tucked away behind the scenes, they were not necessarily downtrodden. Some of their jobs, such as that of cook, were very skilled and very highly regarded. The cook received the highest wages in the kitchen, except for the clerk of the kitchen, who was responsible for the kitchen accounts. Certainly cooks then did not have a reputation for allowing themselves to be downtrodden, any more than they do today. John Russell in his *Book of Nurture* comments on his role as Usher and Marshal:

> For we may allow and dissalow
> Oure Office is the cheeff
> In cellere and spicery
> And the Cooke, be he loothe or leeff.[1]

Russell wrote his book of instructions on how to perform various offices in a great household at the end of a long career spent working for Humphrey, Duke of Gloucester, the illegitimate brother of Henry IV. Evidently his long experience had brought him into conflict with cooks. You can't help wondering what the cook would have said if he had written a similar book.

There seems to have been a degree of flexibility among the lower servants. If there was a job to do, and you were free to do it, then you did it. For example, in 1478 one of Sir William Stonor's gardeners is recorded as making candles.[2] This was a reasonably skilled job, as lots of different grades of candles were used in a large household and the beeswax necessary to make the more prestigious candles was expensive.

John Russell, in his *Book of Courtesy*, describes the office of chandler,[3] whose role was to oversee the household's lighting requirements. He mentions torches, tapers and prickets. Torches were the most significant, being thick candles about a metre long, designed to be carried on the end of a wooden shaft. They would only be used by the most important people in the household, such as the lord himself. Prickets were a less valuable type of candle, but would still have been used by the more important officers of the household. They were made of wax but were much smaller than torches, probably about 2.5cm in diameter. Lesser-grade candles were made of tallow (animal fat). This was much cheaper than beeswax but tended to smoke and give off an unpleasant smell. This is no doubt why Russell reminds the chandler that only wax candles were to be used in the lord's chamber. Certainly making tallow candles must have been a smelly, unpleasant job and perhaps it was this that the unfortunate gardener was called in to do.

The flexibility expected of servants was certainly not all bad news. It could even work in their favour as it could bring talent to the lord's notice. It wasn't only the wealthy and well bred who could rise through service in a household. People of peasant and yeoman stock also rose to high positions. Sometimes this could take generations, as in the case of the Jagons, who served the Earls of Oxford as gardeners and stable hands.[4] By 1513 one member of the family entered the household of the 14th Earl as a caterer, that is, an official responsible for buying supplies for the household. The job entailed considerable financial responsibility. Others rose more swiftly. William Wistowe and William Chomeley both climbed from obscurity to the highest office in the Stafford household through their ability in accounting, which seems to have been the best path to success in the household for those who were not well bred. It is possible that lords even preferred to employ the less well bred in some positions. As we shall see in chapter 6, they often had their own lands and business concerns to deal with, which meant they sometimes had to leave service to attend to them. Men like Wistowe and Chomeley, on the other hand, could dedicate their entire lives to the lord's concerns.

It is difficult to trace individual servants or to learn very much about them. Official records were rarely made of ordinary people in the sixteenth century and many of the records that were made don't survive. Extant records do allow us to build up a general picture of the kind of lives the lower servants led, though it is of course only possible to generalise.

Sleeping accommodation for domestic servants varied. More important servants were often given a private room. Sir John Fastolf's cook had one at Caister Castle in Norfolk as early as 1448. Other servants were not so lucky, and slept where they worked. Also at Caister the bakehouse contained a mattress, blanket, sheet and coverlet, presumably for the bakehouse staff, but at least their quarters would have been warm in the winter. An exception seems to have been made in the case of the kitchen staff, certainly in the royal household. As we shall see, the lowly scullions in Henry VIII's household had been allowed to fall into bad habits. One of the things they were forbidden to do under new ordinances brought in as part of the measures designed to clean up both the kitchen and the scullions themselves was to 'lie in the nights and dayes in the kitchens or ground by the fire-side'.[5] Where they did sleep after that is uncertain, but doubtless it wasn't as warm and cosy as the kitchen.

If Sir John Falstolf's house was typical, the lower servants seem to have enjoyed a reasonable level of comfort. The gardeners' chamber contained two mattresses, a pair of sheets, two blankets, an old carpet, three coverings or coverlets and a celure (a canopy over the bed).[6] Mattresses were often very large, enabling several people to sleep on them at once. John Russell's *Book of Courtesy* even describes the etiquette to be used when asked to share a bed. It was polite to ask the other person which side of the bed they wanted to sleep on, and to sleep as far away from them as possible.[7]

When it came to meals, indoor domestic servants whose jobs were reasonably clean would eat in the great hall. Outdoor servants usually ate where they worked, as the magnificent effect of the lord's household at dinner would be rather spoiled by seriously dirty workmen. The kitchen staff ate in the kitchen, as obviously they would be too busy to eat during the service of dinner. As these two groups made up the greater part of the domestic staff there can't have been many servants dining in the hall, but this is not to say that the hall would be empty. As we shall see later, visitors of one kind or another were both frequent and numerous and often ate in the hall.

While the likes of Thomas Tusser and Gervase Markham debated the rights and wrongs of giving breakfast to servants lower down society, the grander households seem to have decided that menial staff worked best without it. Early in the fifteenth century the ordinances for the running of the household of Edward IV's mother had declared, 'breakfasts be there none, savinge onely the head officers when they be present; to the ladyes and gentlewomen, to the Deane and to the Chappell, to the Almoner, to the gentlemen ushers, to the Cofferer, to the Clerke of the Kitchin and to the Marshall'.[8] Even then it was clear that work came first. Those responsible for accounting ('brevement') had to take their breakfast in the counting house, but only after the accounts had been made up. Dinner and supper were the only two meals that the whole household could expect.

We do have an idea of the kind of food the lower servants ate. Servants' food was considered part of their pay, so the court regulations at this time give sample menus for the different classes of courtier, right down to the lower servants. The less prestigious yeoman servants of the court were given roast beef, veal, lamb or coney (rabbit) at both dinner and supper, plus an allowance of bread and ale. On fish days they were served with ling or cod, plus plaice and whiting. This was plain fare compared to the luxurious dishes which went to the upper courtiers, but good food for someone of their rank at the time.[9] Those at the very bottom of the court ladder, described as 'servants, children of the offices, porters and skowerers' in the court regulations, were served beef, veal or mutton, which was presumably boiled rather than roasted. Roasting is only suitable for the more tender, and therefore the more expensive, cuts of meat. As a consequence, roasted meats were more prestigious and so were considered too good for lowly servants. They had ling and lower quality fish on fish days, although of course they had a bread and ale allowance too. This must have seemed very poor to them in comparison to the more elaborate dishes given to the higher ranks, but it was a very good diet compared with that of those living outside the court.[10]

Table manners were considered very important, and the etiquette books written for children at this time go into great detail about how a polite diner behaved. A lord's great hall at mealtimes would not have been like something out of a Hollywood film, with food being thrown around and generally ending up all over the place. Meals were usually served to the less important in communal portions or messes. Each mess was usually expected to serve four people, and table manners were designed to allow people to share dishes politely and conveniently. For example, you touched communal food only with your left hand, but your own food only with your right hand. It was rude to leave your spoon in the communal dish of pottage as it hindered other people trying to eat. Sharing cups was becoming less common by the sixteenth century, but it still remained polite to empty your mouth and wipe your lips before drinking, so as not to get crumbs in the cup.[11]

On the other hand, perhaps real life did not live up to these ideals. The *Ship of Fools* was first published in Germany in the fifteenth century, but by 1509 it had been translated into English and published in England, and it remained popular throughout the century and indeed into the seventeenth century. It satirises all manner of people in society, from parents who refused to take care in bringing up their children, to men who were constantly running after women. One of its targets is terrible table manners. Perhaps the temptation to grab the best bits of the food on offer was sometimes just too great:

> Some pull from theyr felawes with hande rauysshynge
> And from that mease that nere to them doth syt
> They taste the swettest and best of every thynge.[12]

From this it is easy to see why good table manners were drummed into young ladies and gentlemen at such an early age. Bad habits, such as the grabbing and gobbling commented on here, suggested not only lack of breeding but an unwholesome display of the sin of gluttony.

Servants in great households were also clothed by their employers. This made sense, as shabbily dressed servants would hardly give an impression of wealth and power. As you would expect, the more prestigious the position, the better the clothes that went with it. The lower-grade servants were usually given clothes that were designed to be practical, rather than for display. In the household of Sir William Petre, secretary to Henry VIII, the ordinary servants were given new clothes in the spring and autumn. In the winter they wore grey frieze, a coarse woollen cloth. In the summer they wore grey marble, which was a parti-coloured worsted, woven so that it resembled the veining in marble.[13]

Those who worked hidden away from the public gaze could end up very ill dressed indeed, even in royal circles. The royal scullions (or galapines) mentioned above were so badly dressed that the ordinances declared their clothing a health hazard. The three royal cooks were given 20 marks a year to provide them with 'honest and whole course garments, without such uncleanesse as may be the annoyance of those by whom they shall passe'. The scullions themselves seem to have been suspect characters, as at the same time it was ordained that in future only those who had a reasonable chance of becoming cooks should be taken on.[14] In 1541 the chief cook was given £50 to buy clothes for the thirty-three galapines for the next year.

Servants who were on display could expect far more impressive clothes and were often given liveries made of cloth which the sumptuary laws forbade them to wear. This was another perk of life in a great household, since livery was a reflection of the lord, rather than the person wearing it. This allowed the lord's servants to wear clothes far above their station and their pockets openly and with pride. The sumptuous nature of the livery was important to a lord's status. George Cavendish, Cardinal Wolsey's gentleman usher, describes with great delight how Wolsey's gentlemen wore livery coats of 'Crmmosyn velvet of the most purest Colour that might be Invented', while even his yeomen 'and other mean officers ware in Cottes of ffynne Skarlett garded wt blake velvet an hand brode'.[15] Admittedly the cardinal was making a special effort at the time as he was on embassy to the Emperor Charles V, but it demonstrates how fine livery could get. Certainly lesser servants would never wear fine scarlet (a very fine quality wool) under other circumstances.

Despite the sorry state of the royal scullions, it would be a mistake to think that most lower servants were wallowing in dirt all the time. Andrew Boorde, one of Henry VIII's doctors, wrote a guide to good health known as a 'Dyetary of Helth'. It included advice on everything from healthy eating to building a healthy house. He reminds people 'of all thynges, let the buttery, the celler, the kitchen, the larder-howse, with all other howses of offices be kept clene, that there be no fylth in them, but good and odferous sauours'. Of course, theory and practice are not always the same, but it is of note that the royal scullions had the duty of sweeping and cleaning the 'courts, outwards gallerys and other places of the court, soe as there remaine no filth or uncleanesse in the same'. A dirty palace was hardly going to impress, after all.[16]

Keeping a large house clean was not an easy job. People had to go to the toilet somewhere. The lodgings of the grander members of the household might have their own private garderobe, but other facilities had to be provided for the less fortunate members of the household. Andrew Boorde recommended including 'howses of easementes' as part of a service courtyard, putting them furthest away from the house. The same courtyard would also contain a stable for riding horses but he was careful to add that the courtyard should be kept very clean, with stable dung being carried well away from the house. He also recommended that toilets should be built over water if possible, as this would flush away the debris. Many fashionable sixteenth-century houses had moats around them, but these were not to become sewers. Boorde reminds people that moats had to be cleaned frequently, and kept clear of rotting matter such as kitchen waste.[17]

Again theory is one thing, but was this advice put into practice? Large communal toilets like the one suggested by Boorde were by no means unusual. Whittington's Longhouse, a public toilet built in London with money left specifically for the purpose by Richard Whittington, had no fewer than sixty-four seats.[18] At Hampton Court Palace Henry VIII added a house of easement in the shape of a multi-seated toilet, which was large enough for fourteen people to use at once. It was situated in a wing of the palace which was built out over the moat, but it didn't empty into it. Instead, it emptied into shafts that were flushed with moat water into the nearby River Thames.[19]

All this suggests far more order and cleanliness than we might imagine, but that is not to say that such houses would have met modern hygiene standards. It must often have been a long walk to the common house of easement, and you might have to queue when you got there. Given that great households were mostly male, many were obviously tempted to find somewhere nearer to hand. 'Permit no common pyssing place be aboute the howse or mansion,' warns Andrew Boorde, 'and beware of the emptynge of pysse pottes and pyssing in chymnes. . . .'[20] He evidently knew what he was talking about. Even palaces were not exempt from the problem. At Greenwich, Henry VIII's most used palace, the walls of the inner

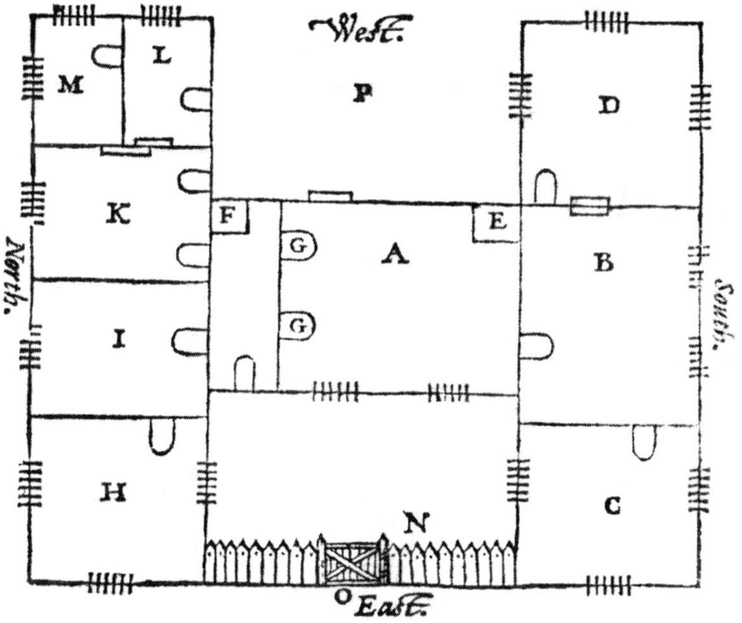

A.	Signifieth the great hall.
B.	The dining parlour for entertainment of strangers [visitors].
C.	An inward closet within the parlour for the mistress' use, for necessaries.
D.	A stranger's lodging with the parlour.
E.	A staircase into the rooms over the parlour.
F.	A staircase into the goodman's rooms over the kitchen and buttery.
G.	The screen in the hall.
H.	An inward cellar within the buttery, which may serve for a larder.
I.	The buttery.
K.	The kitchen, in whose range may be placed a brewing lead, and convenient ovens, the brewing vessels adjoining.
L.	The diary house for necessary business.
M.	The milkhouse.
N.	A fair sawn pale before the foremost court.
P.	A place where a pump would be placed to serve the officers of the house.

This figure signifieth the doors of the house.

This figure signifieth the windows of the house.

This figure signifieth the chimneys of the house.

Gervase Markham's plan for the ideal husbandman's house, published in his *The English Husbandman* (1613), chapter 2 ('of the situation of the Husbandman's house, the necessaries thereto belonging, together with the model thereof').

The perils of bad manners, illustration from *The Ship of Fools*, translated into English by Alexander Barclay, showing 'immoderate vylenes, in maners, vsyd at the table'. *(2286 f. 7 © The British Library)*

Every wealthy person's nightmare – untrustworthy servants. Corrupt cooks and butlers from *The Ship of Fools*. *(2286 f. 7 © The British Library)*

Christopher Hatton's social skills combined with talent brought him considerable success at court. *(Getty Images)*

An early Tudor schoolroom. The schoolmaster ominously clutches his birch. From a supplement to the *Sarum Hymnal*, STC 16111, London, R. Pynson, 1496.

Watercolour of a fortunate housewife, rich enough to own a horse, on her way to market. *(By permission of the Folger Shakespeare Library)*

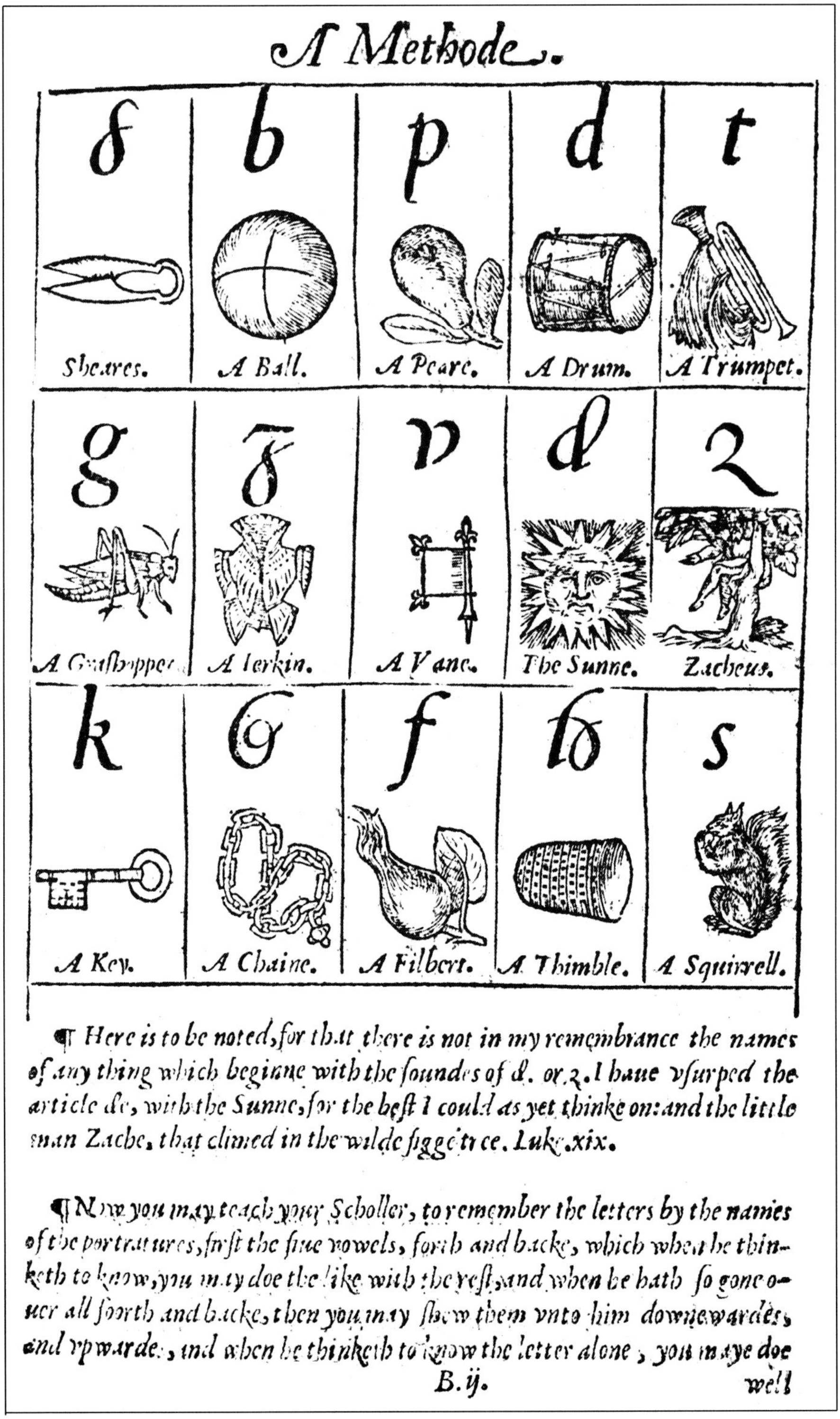

A Methode.

δ	b	p	d	t
Sheares.	A Ball.	A Peare.	A Drum.	A Trumpet.
g	ʒ̄	v	ꝺ	ʓ
A Grashopper.	A Ierkin.	A Vane.	The Sunne.	Zacheus.
k	ɕ	f	ƀ	s
A Key.	A Chaine.	A Filbert.	A Thimble.	A Squirrell.

¶ Here is to be noted, for that there is not in my remembrance the names of any thing which beginne with the soundes of ꝺ. or ʓ. I haue vsurped the article de, with the Sunne, for the best I could as yet thinke on: and the little man Zache, that climed in the wilde figge tree. Luke. xix.

¶ Now you may teach your Scholler, to remember the letters by the names of the portratures, first the fiue vowels, forth and backe, which when he thinketh to know, you may doe the like with the rest, and when he hath so gone ouer all forth and backe, then you may shew them vnto him downewardes, and vpwardes, and when he thinketh to know the letter alone, you maye doe

B.ij. well

A Tudor attempt to make learning more interesting and therefore more accessible. This pictorial alphabet is from John Harte's *Methode or comfortable beginning for all unlearned, whereby they may bee taught to read English* (1570). *(© The British Library)*

A milkmaid, from the *Roxburghe Ballads*, ed. Charles Hindley (London, 1874), ii, p. 16. Her sensible, practical clothes are a world away from the excesses of court dress. *(Mary Evans Picture Library)*

The hard reality of life at harvest time, from the *Roxburghe Ballads*, ed. Charles Hindley (London, 1874), ii, p. 182. A man and woman hard at work in the fields. The couple behind them have taken time off for a little recreation. *(Mary Evans Picture Library)*

Elizabeth I's ladies busy themselves attending their mistress at a christening at which the queen was godmother. *(By permission of The College of Arms, London)*

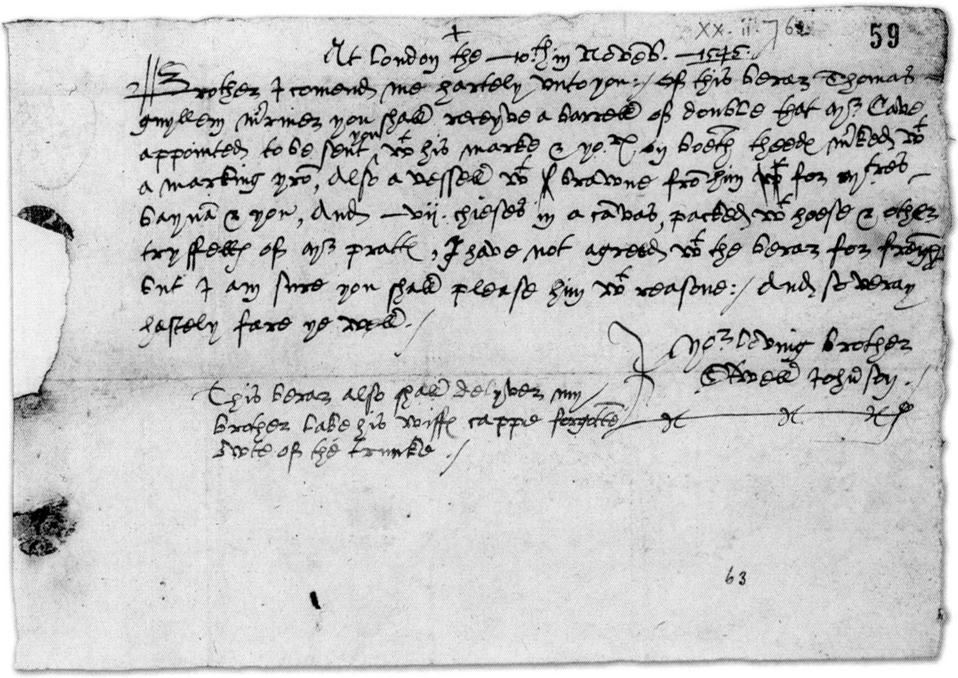

XX. ii. 76 59

At London the 10th in Novemb. 1545

Brother I comend me hartely unto you: of this berar Thomas [illegible] marrinor you shall receyve a barrell of double that mres Cave appointed to be sent you with his marke & yor [illegible] in bothe heede marked wt a marking yron, also a vessell wt the crowne fro him [illegible] for mres Baynam & you, and vij. chesses in a cabas, packed wt [illegible] & other tryfles of mres [illegible], I have not agreed wt the berar for fraight but I am sure you shall please him wt reasone: And so I beare hastely fare ye well.

Yor loving brother
Otwell Johnson.

This berar also shall delyver my brother Cave his wiffe cappe [illegible] [illegible] of the trunke.

63

One of the letters of the Johnson family, now in The National Archives. *(SP1/210 f. 63. By Permission of The National Archives)*

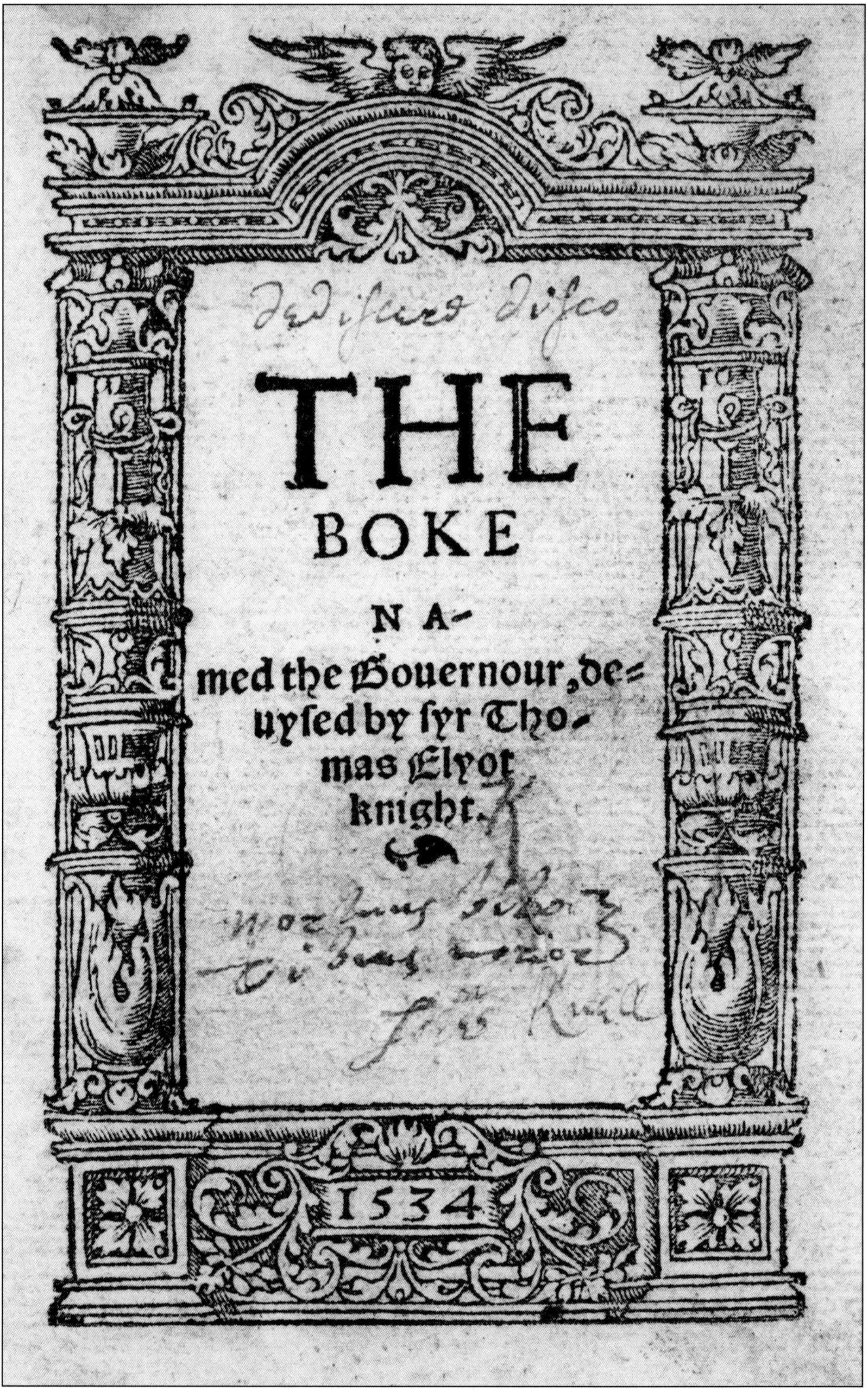
THE BOKE NA-
med the Gouernour, de-
uysed by syr Tho-
mas Elyot
knight.

1534

Thomas Elyot's *The Governor*, a book which greatly influenced Tudor education among the upper classes. *(© The British Library)*

court were plastered and red crosses painted on the plaster. The idea was that nobody would wish to show disrespect by relieving themselves on a cross. Special urinals, which emptied into the sewers, were also provided in the courtyard to control the problem.[21]

Personal hygiene is more of a mystery. Bathing at the time was not a straightforward business. Very rich and important people, such as the monarch, had proper fully plumbed bathrooms with piped water, but this was a very grand option. The usual alternative was to use a wooden bath tub, which looked rather like a barrel cut in half. This would be lined with sheets, so that the person bathing wouldn't get splinters from the rough wood, and they would sit on a stool in the water. There was usually a canopy over the bath to keep out draughts, which were thought to be extremely dangerous to the bather's health. Filling such a bath with hot water was an awkward business, so this was only an option for people who had servants rather than for servants themselves.

Even the very rich did not bath as frequently as we do now. Andrew Boorde again cautioned against too much bathing, warning that it 'allowed the venomous airs to enter and destroyeth the lively spirits in man and enfeebleth the body'.[22] The only kind of washing that we know went on very frequently was the washing of hands before and after meals.

When it came to washing clothes, things were different. In the sixteenth century everyone wore a linen shirt or smock next to their skin, while most people's outer clothes were made of wool. The linen layer was worn for both comfort and hygiene, as at that time woollen clothes could not be washed. Even washing linen was a long process compared to today, so a great deal less washing of clothes went on at that time. Richer people were generally cleaner than poorer ones. In 1501 two henchmen, Anthony Woodville and Edmund Berners, attended the Duke of Buckingham in London. Between them they had eleven shirts washed over a period of eight weeks (3 July–21 August) and another six in the next three weeks. The duke himself had sixteen shirts, six head-kerchiefs, and five pairs of linen sheets washed in a seven-week period.[23] It is difficult to know how typical the duke and his henchmen were. John Russell in his *Boke of Curtesy* suggests that a nobleman should have clean underwear every time he dressed[24] but this could have been the ideal rather than the norm. Either way, it seems that the lower domestic staff would have been lucky to have had a clean shirt every week.

Ironically, the table linen was probably a great deal cleaner. John Russell warns the pantler or butler, who was in charge of the table linen, that the napery should be 'sweet and clean'.[25] Stained, dirty table linen would hardly add dignity to the service of dinner. At court even the linen for the great hall, the least prestigious public dining space, was washed at least twice a week, and more often if it got dirty.

Keeping the house and its occupants clean was obviously important, but it was just as vital to maintain standards of discipline. There was always the danger of fights breaking out in a virtually all-male institution at a time when violence was never far from the surface. As John Russell's instructions for polite behaviour at meal times reminds us: 'In peace though eat and ever eschew/To quarrel at board – that may thee rue',[26] suggesting that such quarrels were not uncommon. In any case discipline was taken seriously and numerous rules and regulations still exist to give an impression of what was and was not allowed.

The chief servants, especially the steward and the marshal, were responsible for keeping the servants in order. Troublemakers were usually sent to them to be 'admonished' or punished in some way. The marshal of the hall had the job of stopping fights in the grandest households. Less elevated households rarely employed such a man, but very likely the job was done by the chief gentleman usher.[27]

Judging from various generations of royal ordinances, and ordinances of the households of various members of the royal family, there were strict conditions to be met. Servants were supposed to be of good character. Stealing, as you would expect, was punished, but Edward IV's ordinances also forbade 'muche haunting of sclaunderous places, companies, and other'. In days when drinking the water was dangerous, it was impossible to ban drinking, but being a 'commyn dayly drunkyn man' was very much forbidden.

Given how quickly disagreements could lead to fights, there were also frequent calls for servants to stay away from arguments, avoiding 'seditious language, varyaunces, discentions, debates and frayes'.[28] It was perhaps for the same reason that gambling was generally forbidden, although traditionally it was allowed during the twelve days of Christmas, when many of the usual rules were relaxed. Swearing was also discouraged. At Edward IV's court it was particularly forbidden to swear by the mass.

Other ordinances were designed to keep the household itself clean and tidy. It was possible to get food from the kitchen between meals, and some people even had an allowance of food which was deliberately intended for eating as snacks. It was very tempting to leave such food lying around, encouraging mice and rats. Doubtless the kitchen also got annoyed at the number of plates that went missing. In Henry VIII's time this was becoming such a problem at court that an ordinance was made against it. No 'manner of dishes, platters, saucers or broken meate' were to be left lying around, but were to be taken back to the squillery, where the washing up was done. The waste food was to be given to the poor by the officers of the almonry.[29]

The punishments for disobedience varied according to the offence, but they hardly seem to have been draconian. In most cases a first offence merely led to a telling off by the head officers of the household. A second offence usually led to loss of wages or of meals. A third offence was far more serious. The offender could lose his job and be thrown out of the household. Under Edward IV the third step was to be put in prison for a month and it was only on the fourth offence that you were sent away from the court in disgrace.

Given the amount of work that the menial servants did there must have been fairly strict discipline in most great households just to get everything done. Large numbers of people came and went, the important ones bringing with them attendants and servants who all had to be fed and housed according to their station. Just how much coming and going there was can be seen from the household of Sir William Petre, Principal Secretary of State. His household at

Ingatestone Hall in Essex comprised about forty people but often had to cope with as many visitors as full-time occupants. The comings and goings in the late 1540s and 1550s give an idea of what the servants of the great had to be able to cope with.

In October 1548 Lord Rich, who was on his way to London, arrived for dinner and probably stayed the night with the thirty persons in his entourage. In November of the same year Princess Mary came, and the servants had to cope with about fifty guests. Early in February 1550 there was another visit from Princess Mary, who came over from nearby New Hall to congratulate Lady Petre on the birth of her son John.

The guests did not stop coming when Sir William was away at court. Lady Petre often played the hostess in her husband's absence. In July 1552 she entertained people varying from Cecil and his wife to Lady Norwich and Mr Tyrell. There were large numbers of other less prestigious visitors too, such as the servants of neighbouring families who came on business, and various craftsmen, from a tailor to a wheelwright and sawyer, all of whom were fed while they were working for the family. In the mid-winter months of 1551/2 there was an average of forty 'strangers' (i.e. people who didn't normally live in the household) at meals and in the following summer and autumn an average of eighty.[30]

A great household was therefore part household, part hotel. Many of the guests expected the best and so the skills of the domestic staff in providing the very finest food and drink were quite considerable. The greatest lords would also provide entertainments to rival those of the court and their wardrobe departments could fit out not only their houses but their lords in quite stunning fashion. The Duke of Buckingham appeared at the Field of Cloth of Gold in 1520 wearing a fabulous outfit covered in little silver bells. The entire process of making this outfit, and those of his equally fabulously dressed attendants, had been carried out in his household, from the initial design, obtaining the fabric and making up.[31]

In the same way noble kitchens could produce the most amazing food. In the highest circles food in the sixteenth century was expected not only to taste wonderful but also to look impressive. This called for incredible skill on the part of the kitchen staff and relied on a complicated system for buying and storing food. Of course at this time you had to organise yourself well in advance, as many types of food were only available in season and storing fresh food was very difficult. Keeping a large household not only fed but fed in a style befitting its lord was not an easy matter and cost a great deal of money. The Duke of Buckingham spent £2,061 on food and drink in 1503–4, although that sum included food for the households of his wife and son, and his own foreign household.[32] The whole system demonstrates the high level of skill and organisation within a great household.

It was the job of the caterer to buy in supplies. The caterer was an important man, with a great deal of financial responsibility, and his position could be easily turned to his advantage. The royal purveyors who supplied the court with various produce were known for their corruption.[33] This was especially problematic at court, where the sheer scale of the supplies needed and the complicated purchasing system used made fraud easy enough. Lords' households were on a much smaller scale and therefore easier to control.

The fact that everything to do with supplying a large household was carefully controlled is important. The impression we have of great households is that expense was no object, and that somehow lavish food and drink were dispensed without thought. This was exactly the image that great lords of the time wanted to create, but the whole effect had to be carefully stage-managed if the family were not to be driven to bankruptcy. Looking at surviving household records it becomes immediately obvious that every penny was accounted for. The kitchen accounts include tiny details, such as how many loaves were baked and how many served. Some of the more detailed kitchen accounts also include lists of guests, so that you could more easily verify what was served and eaten. These controls were evidently very necessary, as dishonest servants seem to have been something of a joke at the time. The *Ship of Fools* had plenty to say about 'folisshe cokes and buttelers and other officers of howsholde that wast theyr maysters goods without mesure'. Though they appeared innocent and trustworthy, once their masters went to bed everything changed:

> Wham mayster and maystres in bed ar to rest
> The bordes are spred, the dores open echone
> Than farys the Coke and Butteler of the best
> Other both together, oreche of them alone
> With wyne and ale tyll all the best be gone
> By gallons and potels they spende without care
> That which theyre lorde for his owne mouth dyd spare.

No wonder kitchen accounts were expected to be so detailed and why so many household ordinances state that food and drink were only to be issued at certain times of the day.

Of course, not all the supplies had to be bought, as very often produce grown on the lord's own lands was used by his household. In the case of livestock, the animals were kept alive for as long as possible and brought on the hoof to wherever the household happened to be. Most great houses had a slaughterhouse attached to them, well away from the main residence, but in 1501 the Duke of Buckingham hired a slaughterhouse at Southwark and a butcher to kill some of his animals to feed his household at Queenhithe.[34] Equally a great lord's deer park was not only a recreational facility, but also a larder.

The meat for most diners was either roasted or boiled. The job of roasting meat was more skilful than might first appear. The meat had to be kept at the right distance from the fire and turned carefully and evenly, and it also had to be frequently basted. It may not have been the most interesting job but it was one which required constant attention and therefore was a good first task to give to a young man newly arrived in the kitchen. Depending on the fireplace, it could also be an uncomfortable job, as it involved being very close to the fire. The heat probably explains why the royal scullions went around wearing very little. The job of boiling was easier. It was usually done in a large built-in boiler known as a lead, which was actually made of copper lined with tin to prevent the copper reacting with the food. The lead was filled with water in the morning, and heated with a fire built underneath it.[35]

The large amounts of fish eaten at this time created more of a problem. First of all fresh fish was a challenge to keep. The royal court was supplied with fresh sea fish by a contractor in Kent who sent it up from the coast in panniers carried by packhorses. Freshwater fish was easier as it could be caught locally, or even bred in fishponds on the lord's estates. Fish was cooked over the coals of the fire on gridirons, or poached in stock over a low fire.[36]

The dishes that were intended for the more important members of the household and guests of suitable rank included elaborate sauces that could not be cooked over the fire. A more gentle, constant source of heat was needed, which was where the use of stoves came in. Built of masonry and fuelled with charcoal, stoves enabled cooks to do the more delicate work. And the need for such work becomes immediately obvious when looking at the kind of food important people expected. Henry VIII's court ordinances, known as the Eltham Ordinances, again give sample menus. The following was the dinner menu on a meat-eating day for senior members of the royal household, such as the gentlemen of the privy chamber, the clerk of the kitchen or the masters of the household. Of course, in addition they also had a bread allowance and ale and wine to drink:

> First Course: Beef, Mutton, Veal, Capons, Coneys, Fryaundes.
> Second course: Lamb, chicken or pigeon, Cocks or plovers, Tart, Fruit, Butter.

As food was considered part of your pay it is reasonable to assume that such a dinner was deemed fitting for men of rank, and thus was the sort of meal that the lord's staff would be expected to prepare for their master and more important members of the household on a regular basis. The above menu sounds plain to the modern ear, but that is because the fine sauces and finishing touches expected from the kitchen were so taken for granted that they were not recorded in the Eltham Ordinances.

For some clue as to the range of sauces available we can turn to John Russell. When describing the duties of the carver he also explains the various sauces that must be served with each dish. Some are fairly straightforward, such as mustard with boar brawn, and verjuice (a rather tart liquid made from sour fruit such as crab apples) with boiled capon, veal, chicken or bacon. Other sauces were more complicated, such as chawdron sauce, which Gervase Markham in his *Complete Housewife* calls a galantine. This was intended for larger fowl, such as swan. The blood of the bird was boiled until thick, then a large quantity of vinegar and a few fine breadcrumbs were added. It was flavoured with sugar and cinnamon and served up in saucers 'as you do mustard'. This was the sort of sauce for which the cook needed the more gentle, controlled heat of the stove.

The menu given above shows that the kitchen was also expected to prepare sweet dishes, at least for the upper household. As sugar was so expensive, being given such dishes was an important status symbol. Certainly attention was drawn to tarts, as they were often works of art. Francis Bacon in his essay 'Of Gardens' comments that he dislikes the very elaborate patterns that were made using various coloured earths in the knot gardens of the time, dismissing them as 'but Toyes. You may see as good Sights, many times, in Tarts.'[37] Given the very elaborate nature of Elizabethan gardens this must have meant a great deal of work in the kitchen.

The butter listed in the menu was sweetened butter, designed to be eaten with a spoon rather than spread on bread. The nearest modern equivalent would be brandy butter.

Given the huge amount of work it is not surprising that even the very grandest of households sometimes had to have extra help. This would particularly have been the case with confectionery. At the very lavish end of the scale confectionery became a combination of dessert, entertainment and artwork. As might be expected, Cardinal Wolsey, who turned going over the top into an art form, provides us with many examples. Cavendish describes a famous entertainment given by the cardinal for the French ambassador. In this case there was a huge amount of sugar work, including a model of St Paul's Cathedral, assorted birds and beasts, a huge array of figures and a chessboard. The chessboard was a particular hit, as the French were considered to be especially good chess players. Cardinal Wolsey even went so far as to present it to one of the French gentlemen, even ordering that a leather case should be made for it so it could be safely carried to France.[38]

Such a profusion of elaborate sugar work was not the norm, even at court. If a nobleman did feel the need to provide such things, he would have hired special confectioners for the occasion, as there wouldn't have been enough work for them on a regular basis. The royal household, on the other hand, did have its own confectionery, staffed with a sergeant, a yeoman confectioner, a groom to assist him and a packhorse man who transported any goods the confectionery needed.[39]

The scale and magnificence of the court required such extravagance. In households such as the Petres', Lady Petre and her daughters themselves may well have made the sugared spices and suchlike required for small-scale entertaining, as skills in confectionery-making were considered a ladylike accomplishment at this time. On the other hand it was perfectly possible to buy in confectionery. 'An hundred marchpane bread' (marchpane was a kind of marzipan) appears on the list of items bought for the wedding of Catherine Tyrell, the stepdaughter of Sir William Petre, in 1552. A quarter ounce of gold leaf, which was most likely used for guilding the marchpane, was also bought.[40] Lower down the scale Sabine Johnson, the wife of a merchant at the Staple, bought in sugared spices costing about a shilling a pound. Considering the cost of the sugar and the spices, this was quite a reasonable price.[41] It must certainly have been a more welcome option than spending hours making your own.

Extra kitchen staff of one kind or another were usually brought in for the greatest occasions. In Sir William Petre's household extra help had to be brought in to cook for Catherine Tyrell's wedding.

A master cook was brought down from London, complete with four under-cooks. As they had to cater for about four hundred people you can understand why they needed extra help. There was even more work as a large number of guests were staying in the house and had to be fed before and after the wedding. On the day before the wedding the guests at dinner alone consumed 4 ling, 4 couple of haberdins,[42] 16 mackerel, 2 conger eels, 15 couple of soles, a thornback, 2 pikes, 4 mullets, 40 flounders, 4½lb of butter, a lead of cheese (that is, 56lb) and 20 eggs. Considering the workload, it is amazing they made do with only five extra kitchen staff.

Sometimes even royal facilities could not cope with the really grand occasions. At Greenwich Palace a special new working-house was built for the master cooks to prepare the Twelfth Night banquet in 1533.[43]

In general, life in a great household as a domestic servant seems to have been quite acceptable. You were fed, clothed and housed by your master and, provided you worked hard and stayed out of trouble, there was reasonable job security. If the royal kitchen was typical, then there were opportunities for advancement for the ambitious. There would be the interest of seeing a wide range of people coming and going as guests, and perhaps the excitement of great occasions such as royal visits. Your lot was certainly better than that of domestic servants in less grand houses.

SIX

Henchmen, Honour and Hospitality Gentlemen Servants in a Great Household

A great lord required a large number of gentlemen servants not only to maintain the degree of ceremony considered necessary to his social position but also to entertain visitors in suitable style. As educated men, they were also vital in helping the lord to maintain and run his estates and in forming his administrative team if he held office at court. They were so vital that around a quarter of a great lord's household would consist of gently bred servants. Not all of them were in constant attendance. Some very rarely lived in their lord's household as their duties kept them elsewhere. Others could not always be in attendance as they had their own affairs to look after. The Northumberland Household Book suggests that although a large number of gentlemen servants were employed, only a quarter of them were in attendance at one time.

In this chapter we shall look at the work these people did, starting with the daily ceremonies that some of them were expected to perform.

EVERYDAY CEREMONY

The degree of ceremony that enveloped a lord seems almost unbelievable to modern people. John Russell's *Boke of Nurture*, written around 1460–70, gives an idea of some of the etiquette surrounding an aristocrat. Russell had been usher and marshal to Humphrey, Duke of Gloucester, the illegitimate brother of Henry IV. His book was used as the basis of Wynkyn de Worde's *Boke of Keruynge*, which had gone into its second edition by 1513, so the ideas were still current in the sixteenth century. Lots of young sixteenth-century gentlemen must have been familiar with it, although whether they took quite the same delight in the complicated rituals described therein as John Russell himself did remains open to question.

There is far too much ceremony described by Russell to include here, but a good example of how even the mundane was elaborated can be seen in the etiquette involved in laying tables. At this stage you must imagine that the lord is dining in hall, rather than in private. The first table to be laid was, of course, the table at which the lord would be eating. The first thing to do was to wipe the table. The table would then be laid with three cloths, one over the top of the table, one with its central fold on the outer edge of the table and another with its central fold on the inner edge. At this stage neither the lord himself nor any guests would yet be present, but even so considerable reverence was involved in making ready for his presence. The person setting the table started by putting a long, narrow towel around his neck. Towels at this time were made of linen, often woven with a pattern like tablecloths, and there was no raised pile, such as a modern towel has, so to us this towel would have looked more like a napkin. One end of the towel would then be placed over the left arm, and on this he would place the lord's napkin, and lay eight loaves of bread on it. (Loaves at this time were smaller than most modern ones, so this was less unlikely than it sounds.) Russell also says to add three or four trencher loaves. These four-day-old loaves would end up being used, in effect, as plates, but by the sixteenth century grander households were beginning to replace them with wooden trenchers for ordinary diners, and silver or pewter plates for grander ones. In the next step he picked up the salt cellar with his left hand, and laid the right end of the towel over his right hand in order to pick up the lord's spoons and knives without actually touching them. It was respectful not to touch, or at least touch as little as possible, anything that the lord was going to use. Once he reached the table, everything had to be laid carefully in its place. The lord's spoon, napkin, trencher and knife were then covered up with a napkin.

Everything about the lord's life was raised to similar levels of intricacy. There was ceremony involved in everything from making his bed to dressing him in the morning.[1] A young man who hoped to make a career out of personal service to a lord had to know how to take part in such rituals. One particular area in which he needed to have practical experience was carving meat. This was always performed in public, just as meat is still carved at the table even today. The idea was that meat and fish should be cut in such a way as to produce pieces that looked elegant and pleasing on the diners' plates. However, by Russell's day carving had gone far beyond that and had become extended into an elaborate ritual, with its own technical terms. The carver also had to know what sauce should be served with each dish, so there was a great deal to remember. Knowledge of the ceremony involved was part of a young gentleman's education, so everyone knew how it should be done and his peers were doubtless quick enough to point out any mistakes.

The carver had to have a clean, sharp knife. He was to touch the meat only with his left hand, but this was a practice everyone was accustomed to. (As we have seen, Russell reminds the carver that you touch other people's food only with your left hand and your own only with your right.) There were very definite instructions for carving all the different birds, fish and animals that might be served. Brawn, for example, was cut on the dish and the slices lifted off with the knife. In the case of a fawn, kid or lamb, the kidney was served first, then the carver had to lift up the shoulder, take off a rib, then remove the fyfax (the tendon of the neck). Even pies needed the attention of the carver. Capon, chicken or teal pies had to be taken out of the crust, the wings minced and then stirred into the gravy so that the lord could eat it with a spoon. Venison or boar, on the other hand, was cut in the pastry. Even custards, which we wouldn't think of carving today, were cut into neat squares by the carver so that they could be easily removed from the crust.

Having carved, the carver then had to remember what sauce to serve with each dish. Lamb was served with ginger sauce, for example, but pea soup or frumenty (basically husked and boiled wheat) went with beaver's tail, and so on. The terminology was elaborate, with a whole list of correct terms to learn, such as the fact that you 'broke' venison, 'chyned' a salmon and 'reared' a goose.

Ironically the only elaborate ceremony that the lord may have not had to sit through, depending on his status, was the one that many modern readers presume always took place. There was a genuine fear of poisoning in the sixteenth century, but the elaborate ceremony around testing for it was more a status symbol than a practical test for poison. John Russell declares: 'Tasting is only done for those of royal blood, as pope, emperor, empress, cardinal, king, queen, prince, archbishop, duke or earl.'[2]

To truly understand such rituals, you really needed to be brought up in surroundings where it was all part of daily life. This was one reason why such households were considered excellent places in which to educate well-bred young girls and boys. Although their education took in social etiquette, it also touched on a great deal more than that, and included academic subjects, sport, music and dancing.

THE HENCHMEN

The young gentlemen being educated in a great household were known as 'henchmen'. As we have already seen, gently bred children often did not see very much of their parents. Medieval theorists divided childhood into three parts: *infancia*, which lasted until the age of seven, *puericia* or boyhood, which lasted from seven to fourteen, and *adolescencia*, which lasted from fourteen to twenty-one. For the first seven years children would generally be in the care of women, their mother and a nurse. At around the age of seven boys and girls were often set on different paths. Girls remained under the care of women while boys' education now continued with schoolmasters. Once he reached the age of fourteen a boy moved on to higher studies, perhaps even spending a year or two at university, or possibly some time at one of the Inns of Court, which we will look at later.

It is important to point out that there were far fewer hard and fast rules in education at this time than there are today. Children could do different things at different ages, depending on when an opportunity came up or when their parents thought the time was right. It was fashionable to send wealthy young men on educational trips abroad by the end of the sixteenth century, but they did not all go at the same age. William Cecil, Lord Roos (great-nephew to Robert Cecil), went to Paris in 1615 aged sixteen, the same age at which Sir John Harrington went to Florence with his tutor, Mr Tovey. William Lord Cranborne went abroad with his tutor, Matthew Lister, when he was eighteen and Henry, Lord Clifford, when he was nineteen. Edward Herbert, on the other hand, was twenty-five when he went to Paris to finish his education. In the same way the group of children being educated in a household could cover quite a span of age, so that tutors could be teaching children of different ages simultaneously.[3]

There was very little emphasis on passing exams. National examination syllabuses lay far in the future and even at university level many young gentlemen never formally took their degree, but without causing any damage to their future career. Sir Christopher Hatton never formally took his degree at Oxford, yet he rose to be Lord Chancellor in the time of Elizabeth I. Presumably tutors and parents between them decided when the boy had achieved the desired level of accomplishment.

This is not to say that education was taken lightly. It seems that specialist schoolmasters were being increasingly employed in great households to oversee the education of gently bred children. Even earlier, in the Middle Ages, the education of such children had revolved around more than social etiquette, use of arms and the like. The study of music, literature and languages had always been important, so the idea of the 'Renaissance man' able to excel in a variety of fields was a development of an old idea rather than a new one.[4]

A flavour of the curriculum followed by such children can be found in the famous Black Book of Edward IV. The ordinances in it refer to the henchmen of his court and state that there were to be at least six of them, although there could be more, according to the king's wishes. They had a master, whose duties included teaching them how to ride well, how to take part in jousts, how to speak and behave, and how to show due religious observance. He was also to teach them languages, singing, dancing and music, specifically harping and piping.[5] In short, he taught them everything but grammar, which was the domain of a specialist teacher.

We don't have much specific information about the lives of schoolboys in great households, but we do have quite a few clues as to what life was like in Tudor schools generally. From these we can build up a picture of what life would be like for the henchmen. First of all we must forget any idea of long rows of children sitting at desks, as in Victorian schoolrooms. To start with, the classes would have been small by today's standard. Cardinal Wolsey had nine or ten young lords being educated in households in the 1520s, while the Earl of Northumberland had three henchmen and two other young gentlemen 'at their friend's finding' – that is, being educated in the household but paid for by friends or relatives rather than by the earl.[6] Chairs were symbols of authority, and so there was no hope of those for children. They may have sat on benches, or even on the floor at the schoolmaster's feet. A picture of an early Tudor school in a fifteenth-century hymnal shows schoolchildren sitting just like this.

Discipline would have been strict by modern standards, but then Tudor children were generally brought up far more strictly than modern children. Answering back to adults outside school, let alone during school hours, was neither expected nor tolerated. But while the rod was definitely not spared, it would be a mistake to assume that all Tudor schoolchildren were endlessly beaten for no real reason. When beating was used, it was considered to be kind to the child in the long run. It was thought that a beating was the best way of correcting foolish behaviour which would only lead the child into difficulties in later life. An indulgent parent who refused to approve such punishment was seen as irresponsible. Here are some words of advice from a school book, designed to be translated into Latin as an exercise, and intended to remind children that the beatings they received were ultimately for their own good:

> And thus is process of time, when their cum to age, their waxe bolde to do all myschevounes, settynge litell to do the greatest shame that can be. And at the laste, after merites, sum be hangede, sum be hedyde; . . . and whan they cum to that ende, thei curse the father and mothers and other that ade rule of them in ther youghe.[7]

How many were comforted by the fact that their punishment was designed to keep them away from hanging or beheading must remain a mystery.

Of course good teachers in any age know that endless beatings are not an effective teaching aid, and this fact was already acknowledged in Tudor educational theory. Roger Ascham, who was tutor to both Edward VI and Elizabeth I, believed strongly that kindness and encouragement were better aids to education than fear. His book *The Schoolmaster*, published in 1570 after his death, advocated correcting the faults children made in their work by explaining where they had gone wrong, rather than by beating them. He also believed that education should be made as interesting as possible, since boring work was 'tedious for the master, hard for the scholar, cold and uncomfortable for both'.[8] In 1531 Thomas Elyot published *The Governor*, a book that proved to be a best-seller by the standards of its day (running into eight editions by 1580) and something of a standard textbook on education for the sixteenth century. He too calls for the avoidance of cruelty by schoolmasters and the use of praise rather than shame to encourage children.

Surviving school materials do suggest that teachers did try to add fun to lessons. By the end of the sixteenth century writers were increasingly writing in their own native languages, but many learned books were still written in Latin. Anyone who hoped to get a higher education therefore had to learn Latin. As part of the process, pupils would translate various English sentences into Latin. Wooden tablets covered in wax were often used for writing in schools, where the pupil would write in the wax with a stylus. The wax could easily be smoothed over after the work was completed. Fortunately paper was becoming cheaper, so by the fifteenth century it was appearing in schools, and a few of the pupils' notebooks used for lessons have survived.

The books contain a number of exercises done by children, including many sentences translated from English into Latin. The sentences were important in themselves, while the copying itself was considered part of their education, not least because it improved their handwriting. Having good handwriting was very important in the days when all correspondence was handwritten. The sentences were also often aimed at teaching moral lessons, like the one on the importance of beatings given above. However, the teachers also include sentences concerning everyday life, sometimes even with a little touch of humour. A book from Barlinch Priory school has a sentence complaining that he who eats little at supper, lunch, dinner and breakfast has no spirit left in him. In another the writer says that he has eaten as much bacon and egg as he possibly can ('I hawe ete my belyfull of coloppes and egges today'). In another book, one sentence says 'Yff ther be eny of my fellows that love not my maister, I confesse that I am on ('If there be any of my fellows that does not love my master, then I confess that I am one').[9]

If the school day in a great house followed the same pattern as the local school, then it began early. Most schools seem to have opened at six, and in one book five o'clock is mentioned as the starting time.[10] This would make sense, as the boys would be beginning lessons at the same time that the rest of the household commenced their duties. Lessons in great households could be fairly informal, especially as what we would regard as mere leisure pursuits were seen as educational. This was no doubt why John Palsgrave, who was charged with the education of Henry VIII's illegitimate son Henry Fitzroy, Duke of Richmond, complained to Thomas More that the daily routine he was trying to build up with his pupil was constantly disrupted. People were always tempting the young duke away from his studies, 'some to hear a cry at a hare, some to kill a buck with his bow, sometime with greyhounds, sometime with buckhounds . . .'.[11]

Despite these temptations, the evidence suggests that more formality was being introduced and more and more pupils were following strict timetables. Around 1530 Thomas Cromwell's son Gregory had an order of study including French, writing, music and athletics, all defined in terms of hours.

The basis of the academic side of the boys' education at this time was, not surprisingly, the study of Latin and classical literature, and perhaps also ancient Greek. Thomas Elyot even suggested surrounding boys from their earliest years with nurses and other female servants who would speak to them in Latin, but that seems to have been more of an academic ideal than any kind of reality. A nurse who spoke Latin fluently must have been as rare as hens' teeth.

According to Elyot, between the ages of seven and fourteen boys were to study grammar, simple prose and poetry. Between the ages of fourteen and twenty-one they would learn logic, rhetoric, history and geography, plus geometry and astronomy. At seventeen they would start the study of moral and political philosophy, especially the 'wisdom literature' from the Bible, such as the book of Ecclesiastes and the New Testament.

The subject of religious education is an important one. Given the significance of religion in society at the time it is perhaps surprising that the formal study of the subject seems to have been missing from education, at least before the Reformation. The answer to this seems to have been that there was no need to teach it formally as children took it in as part of daily life. The royal henchmen, and presumably other gently bred children living in noble households, were certainly expected to attend daily church services and the normal way to learn to read at the time was by reading from a book of hours or some similar religious book. Latin exercises could also be based on religious books. Gregory Cromwell is mentioned as translating the paternoster and creed from Latin in about 1530.[12]

Despite the emphasis on Latin and sometimes ancient Greek, modern languages were also taught. This could, of course, be an asset at court, where involvement in diplomatic work could lead to advancement, but languages were also seen as a social asset. French and Italian seem to have been the languages most commonly taught. By the mid- to late sixteenth century it was common for noblemen's sons to spend a year or two abroad to learn both the ways of a country and its language. Sir Philip Sidney's educational travels took him to Paris (where he narrowly missed being caught up in the St Bartholomew's Day Massacre), Frankfurt, Heidelberg, Strasburg, Vienna, Hungary, Italy, Germany and Poland. He was away for three years.[13]

From all this it is possible to see that a well-educated young gentleman of the sixteenth century received a good solid academic education, but this was very much only part of the picture. Edward IV's famous Black Book emphasises the fact that the Master of the Henchmen was to sit with his pupils at meal times 'to have his respecte unto theyre demeanynges, howe mannerly the etge and drink, and theyre communication'. In other words he was to supervise their social behaviour as much as their academic life, because the two were equally important.

Tudor educational handbooks always take it for granted that children will be brought up in groups, rather than singly. Even so, children growing up in a great household would be vastly outnumbered by the adults, and would be expected to copy adult behaviour. Books such as John Russell's *Book of Carving* and *Book of Courtesy* also make it clear that young men were expected to take part in the rituals of serving dinner and to know the roles of the different people involved. The idea was not only to teach them the rituals involved, but also to give them the social confidence to play a public role without being overawed by the occasion.

The other advantage of having young gentlemen take part in the rituals of dinner was that it reminded them of their place. They had to understand their social obligations, to both superiors and inferiors. They also had to learn how their families fitted in. Tudor children were not brought up with the idea that they should become independent from their families at a fairly early age. They would be required to show considerable respect to their parents, and especially their father, for as long as they lived. They were also expected to consider themselves part of their family rather than as an independent individual for their entire lives. For example, if success at court were to come their way, they would be expected to use whatever influence they had to obtain jobs and favours for other family members as well as their friends.

Edward IV's Master of the Henchmen was also to teach his charges to have 'all curtesy in wordes, dedes and degrees'. A gentleman had to be constantly aware of how he appeared to others, whether above or below him in social terms, and a nobleman even more so. Even when he was enjoying himself he had to do so in a seemly manner, at least in public. 'Laugh not too oft' was the advice of John Russell; 'Who laughs that all men may him see/A shrew [i.e. wicked man] or fool him seems to be.' A child brought up in a noble household would be expected to know how to behave correctly in all circumstances.

The non-academic parts of the curriculum would also have helped to build confidence, but that was not their only purpose. A Renaissance gentleman was supposed to be a man of action, capable of fighting battles. This involved a great deal of training in order to get fit and to maintain fitness. This was part of the reason for the Tudor obsession with hunting.

Hunting was far more skilled and complicated than people unacquainted with the subject often realise. The mental challenge of planning the chase appealed to many, while the courage and stamina needed to pursue the quarry across country was seen as developing the strength and determination needed on the battlefield. It was also seen as an antidote to idleness, something much feared by sixteenth-century moralists. It was also perfect for Tudor networking, as being asked to join a hunt by a social superior was a great honour. Great lords loved it because keeping deer parks, packs of hounds and all the paraphernalia associated with them cost a considerable amount of money, which of course made them a status symbol. Tudor royalty, especially Henry VIII and Elizabeth I, loved hunting, so it was a wonderful way to entertain them should they be in the area. On top of all this, the game caught could be eaten in the household or sent as a gift to someone in the endless round of gift-giving that was expected of the Tudor well-to-do.

There was a great deal to learn regarding the hunt. It was no surprise that numerous textbooks on hunting were produced, the most famous being the fifteenth-century *Book of St Albans*. From these books young people could memorise what they needed to know to avoid making embarrassing mistakes on the hunting field, such as the meanings of 'the measures of blowing', carefully written in rhyme to make them easier to remember. For example, two short blasts and one long one meant that a buck had been killed with hounds. They also had to learn the complicated terminology. The hart, the male red deer, considered the prime quarry in England, graduated from being a claso, a broket, a spayd, a stag and finally a great stag before it made it to the heights of being called a hart in its sixth year.[14] There was clearly a lot to learn. Doubtless most Tudor boys preferred the practical lessons to learning the theory.

Another practical lesson which Tudor boys seem to have enjoyed a great deal was dancing. Many modern men would run a mile at the thought of dancing lessons but the Tudors felt differently on the subject. Thomas Elyot recommended dancing as a way of maintaining fitness for warfare, as recommended by the ancient Greeks, and certainly there was no sense of dancing being in some way effeminate. Henry VIII himself was an enthusiastic dancer, and being able to dance well at court was pretty much a necessity. There was an added incentive to learning to dance, at least for the older boys. Dancing was one of the few ways in which young men and women could mix freely, so any young man who wanted a healthy social life was well advised to pay close attention to his dancing teacher.

A great deal of the boy's day would also be taken up with various types of training for warfare. Boys were introduced to weapons very young and spent a great deal of time practising to use them. According to Elyot, particular attention was paid to building young men up physically once they turned fourteen, but this does not mean that the academic side of their education was forgotten. In the early seventeenth century Sir Thomas Puckering was attending the famous academy of M. de Pluvinel in Paris. His tutor recorded in a letter that Mr Puckering would start the day with two hours' riding, sometimes from seven until nine and sometimes from nine to eleven. He spent another hour reading in French and another in translating Latin with his tutor. After that he had an hour's fencing lesson, until dinner at twelve. The dinner break lasted until two, although it might also include some other kind of 'honest recreation pertaining to arms'. At two he had an hour's dancing, after which he spent two hours translating from Latin to French with his tutor.[15]

The non-academic part of the curriculum could be as vital as the academic when it came to a gentleman's future career. Sir Christopher Hatton is a good example of how social skills could bring you to royal attention. Hatton came from a lesser gentry family with only modest resources, although he was educated at Oxford and then at the Inner Temple. As we shall see later, the young gentlemen students at the Inns of Court took part in plays and masques, particularly at Christmas. Being close to Whitehall, it was not unusual for royalty to attend. In 1562 it seems that Hatton was taking part in a masque in which Robert Dudley was also appearing, and which was attended by the queen. She was so impressed by his dancing that she decided he would be an ornament to her court, which led to him becoming a gentleman pensioner in 1564.

Hatton's skills did not end with dancing. He was an expert at the joust, a skill long-since outdated on the battlefield, but important for taking part in the elaborate tournaments held at court. More importantly, he excelled at the game of courtly love. Courtly love had a long history, going back into the Middle Ages. It could be a simple matter of romance, with a gentleman wooing his lady to get her into bed, but it was often far more complicated than that and might not involve sex at all. It was really a way by which a gentleman might bring himself to the attention of a lady, perhaps more in the hope that she might use her influence to his advantage, such as helping him to get a job at court, than anything else. Of course in the reign of Elizabeth, all the gentlemen of the court played the game of wooing the queen; Hatton played the game extremely well and does even seem to have developed a genuine friendship with her. He went on to become a gentleman of the privy chamber and captain of the Yeomen of the Guard, and then to be a JP and MP. He also became a privy councillor, and then Lord Chancellor in 1587. Naturally he could hardly have made a suitable Lord Chancellor without a good academic education, but it was his social skills that first brought him to royal attention.[16]

A young gentleman who had finished his education in a grand household would find himself well equipped for life. The social connections and skills he had developed might help him find a position at court, but this was always a difficult option as there was enormous competition for any position suitable for a gentleman. Many boys from such backgrounds hoped for a military career, as training in arms was considered to be especially good in great households. Others might be sent elsewhere to complete their education before starting work. University was one option.

Originally university was the place you went if you were intended for a career in the church, but after the Reformation this began to change. In the second half of the sixteenth century more and more young men spent a year or two at university, although they were much younger than modern university students. George Cavendish, gentleman usher to Cardinal Wolsey, seems to have gone to Cambridge at the age of eleven,[17] although many others were in their early teens. They also went for varying amounts of time. In

1501 Robert Constable provided for his son Marmaduke to be maintained at Cambridge for three years, while in 1505 Thomas Wentworth arranged for his son Thomas to be sent to a grammar school for two years and then to Cambridge for one. As we have seen, many young men never took their degrees. University was frequently seen as a stage in a gentleman's education, rather than the end of it. Wealthy young men might be sent off travelling to complete their education abroad, while many others spent at least a year at one of the Inns of Court afterwards.

The Inns of Court were, then as now, intended for training lawyers. The full training for those intending a career in law was very long indeed, being up to twelve years. While a knowledge of the law was useful, and indeed vital for a gentleman who needed to defend his land but could not afford to use lawyers too much, the main attraction was that the Inns of Court were really seen as a young gentleman's finishing school. They were conveniently placed near Whitehall, where the court was frequently to be found, so that young gentlemen could visit the court to learn its ways. Young men not only studied the law, but also took lessons in fencing, dancing and music. They also put on entertainments such as masques. When the heir of Sir William Fitzwilliam entered Gray's Inn in 1594 his expenditure on music, dancing and fencing lessons amounted to more than the cost of his residence.[18]

One option that would not be open to a young gentleman by the end of the sixteenth century was that of finding work as a gentleman servant. The sad ending of this career opportunity was noted in 1598, when a book was published entitled *A Health to the Gentlemanly Profession of Serving-Men.* The writer let himself be known discreetly by his initials alone, I.M. The book is a long complaint about the fact that the profession is now so badly paid that a gentleman simply could no longer think of following it. The days of service in the great chamber are lost, the aristocracy are served by people of no breeding, and the old ways of great lords living surrounded by flocks of attendants who followed them everywhere are gone. 'I meete a Gentleman that may dipende yearly by his revenues 2,000 pundes of good and lawfull Englysh money, with onely one boy at this heeles . . .', he complains. After this time it was only at court that well-bred ladies and gentlemen would be happy to wait on royalty, maintaining the old tradition of service. As we have seen elsewhere, the great households were declining and, as I.M. noted, by the end of the sixteenth century personal service was no longer a career for a gentleman.

By the late sixteenth century great households were no longer places of education for gentlemen either. The households of the rich remained excellent places for training for the lower social orders, who were happy to be grooms, gardeners, cooks and the like, so their educational function was not entirely lost. But this was hardly the sort of career path that a gentleman wished to set his son upon, so by the later sixteenth century most gentlemen were educated at their local grammar school. The educationist Richard Mulcaster pointed out that this was a far better arrangement, as it was more suitable for gentlemen's sons to mix with what he referred to as 'the common' at a grammar school than to learn inflated ideas of their own importance in a noble household.[19]

The great nobles still employed private tutors but these men were no longer shared with other boys outside the family as they once had been. The gentry and the aristocracy might meet up later on, at university or the Inns of Court, but they were no longer brought up together.

YOUNG LADIES

Young girls were sent into noble households as attendants on the lady of the house. Just like their brothers, they could be sent away from home at different ages, depending on when an opportunity arose. Some were very young when they left home. Thomasine Petre, for example, was sent away to finish her education in the household of the Countess of Exeter when she was only ten. Lady Jane Grey was only nine when she joined Catherine Parr's household. Their education would have been rather different from the education of their brothers. Girls were certainly not brought up to be involved in the elaborate etiquette of serving dinner, for example. Ladies simply did not do that. In illustrations the lady of the house is sometimes seen serving a peacock sitting on a plate as if it were alive, complete with its full complement of feathers. But this was a rare event and in any case seems to have gone out of fashion in the sixteenth century.

The exclusion of girls from these public roles was logical, given the place of women at the time. Gently bred boys were expected to appear confident in society, but ladies were supposed to be modest and unassuming. While a lady was expected to take her place in society with ease, young girls would not have been encouraged to do anything that would make them appear too dangerously confident. The academic education that a well-bred young girl received varied enormously, depending on her parents' feelings on the subject and the atmosphere of the household in which she was brought up. Some were famously well educated, such as Elizabeth I, Lady Jane Grey, and the four Cooke sisters who all married prominent courtiers in Elizabeth I's time. Lady Mary Sidney, Sir Philip Sidney's sister, learnt Hebrew, Greek, Latin, French and Italian. However, such impressive achievements were not the norm. Tudor women were brought up principally to be wives, mothers and managers. Their education was certainly not lacking but in most cases it was primarily practical rather than academic. Even the grandest ladies were not brought up with an ideal of genteel idleness, as was to be the case in the eighteenth and nineteenth centuries.

A well-bred young girl was taught to read but that doesn't mean to say that girls were necessarily encouraged to read anything they could find. J.L. Vives, tutor to Henry VIII's daughter Mary, wrote a book entitled *The Education of a Christian Woman* which was published in 1532 and was very influential in its day. Vives believed that girls should only be allowed to read serious moral writings. For example, if a girl was to read the classics, she was to be kept away from writers such as Ovid, who might lead her into flirtatious ways. How many girls evaded this censorship we will never know, as obviously they would have needed to keep their dangerous reading habits secret.

Just like her brothers, a gently bred girl's time was not taken up entirely with academic education. Generally women spent most of their lives at home on their estates, while their husbands might well be away at court or on business. The day-to-day running of the family business might well end up in the hands of the lady of the house. For example Lady Margaret Hoby, the earliest known woman diarist, records overseeing everything from the weighing of wool and having her honey put in order to discussions around buying a farm. She also mentions evenings spent reading papers relating to business and discussing business with her husband, suggesting that he saw her involvement in the affairs of the family as quite normal.[20]

Grace Sherrington, who later became Lady Mildmay, left reminiscences of her early years spent with her governess, a niece of her father's called Mistress Hamblyn. She seems to have been a more typical young lady than the Cookes or Mary Sidney. She learnt how to cast accounts and how to write a good letter, and also spent a great deal of time learning about medicine either directly from Mistress Hamblyn or from herbals. There were not many doctors around in the sixteenth century and women needed at least some knowledge of medicine to look after their families. If a wealthy lady found herself living in a remote place she had to be able to cope with all kinds of medical emergencies as you simply could not rely on being able to find a doctor.[21]

Although young girls did not take as much physical exercise as their brothers, they were not expected to spend their whole lives sitting about looking demure. Ladies were not, of course, taught how to use weapons like their brothers, but they could still take part in the hunt. Ladies were allowed to learn archery for this purpose, and could become enthusiastic huntswomen. Elizabeth I certainly loved hunting.

Dancing was another important form of exercise. As we have already seen, it was the main way in which the sexes could meet unchaperoned, which was why Vives suggested that girls should not be allowed to dance. But in reality dancing was so much a part of social life that it was impossible to ban girls, while anyone with social ambitions for their daughter knew that skill at dancing was a basic necessity. Hours of practice were needed to master some of the more complicated dances, so this must have been a useful form of exercise.

Despite the fact that girls were not encouraged to look too self-confident in public, part of the reason you sent your daughter to a great household was to gain social polish and to form the right connections, or strengthen existing ones. The right connections are useful in any age but in Tudor times they could mean life or death, or certainly the difference between a life of financial hardship and one of ease. Although women were not allowed to play an open part in politics and were never appointed to positions of political power, the family and social connections of women were often vital in ensuring the success of the families they married into. The importance of a woman's connections can be demonstrated by the struggles of Elizabeth Raleigh, née Throckmorton, widow of Sir Walter Raleigh.

Sir Walter had been convicted of treason in November 1603 but was granted a stay of execution which in the end lasted for thirteen years. A conviction of treason was a particular disaster for a family, because all the convicted person's belongings reverted to the crown, leaving his wife and children penniless. It therefore fell to Elizabeth to try to obtain some kind of economic protection, especially for the estate of Sherborne which had been granted to Raleigh in 1599. Sir Walter himself believed it to be safe because he had gifted it to his son Carew, but a clerical error had ruined his plan. As we shall see later, the paperwork involved in land ownership was unbelievably complicated at this time and such errors were not uncommon.

The whole case shows Tudor and early Stuart society at its worst. Women were very much in men's power, and could do very little to prevent economic exploitation. Elizabeth herself had found this out early in her life. Her father had died when she was only about six, and her mother had foolishly lent her daughter's inheritance of £500 to the Earl of Huntingdon. The money was never recovered.

Elizabeth's attempts to save Sherborne were no more successful than her attempts to regain her inheritance, but they do illustrate the networks of women that existed in the sixteenth century. A letter written in 1604 to Robert Cecil, secretary to James I, shows how she attempted to use this network to regain the estate. The back of the letter appealing to Cecil for help in regaining her land is signed by no fewer than eighteen ladies, some relatives and some friends, adding their weight to Elizabeth's request. These female networks obviously did not have the power of male ones, but they could be all a woman had to rely on in times of need. In any case, although Sherborne was not recovered, Elizabeth's efforts were not in vain. Carew Raleigh was certainly not left a pauper. He later became a courtier, which required reasonable wealth, and was made gentleman of the privy chamber in 1635.[22]

Given the necessity of such connections, we can understand why Tudor parents were so keen to send their children away into other households. We sadly have very little evidence of the personal feelings of those involved, and whether the children went willingly or not. From private letters, though, we do have a few hints of the strains and stresses involved for both parents and children. In the mid-fifteenth century, for example, one of the daughters of Jane Stonor had been placed in a household by no less a patron than the queen herself, Elizabeth Wydeville. Unfortunately the girl did not like the position much, and felt that the owners of the household were weary of her. Jane's reply was not a stinging rebuke, telling the girl to be grateful for the opportunity open to her. Instead, she replied that her daughter could certainly come home, but that the queen must give her approval first. This highlights the point that the parents themselves did not always have free choice as to their child's fate. Parents too were under social obligations that could not always be ignored.

Despite the obedience expected of children, their feelings were not always disregarded. In the early sixteenth century Dorothy, one of

Sir Robert Plumpton's children, was placed in the household of Lady Darcy at Temple Hirst in Yorkshire. Dorothy evidently did not like Lady Darcy very much, and sent a message to her father asking to be called home. Lady Darcy got to hear about it, but instead of being angry, she seems to have solved the problem by talking to Dorothy about the matter. Dorothy's next letter to her father shows that the problem had been solved to everyone's satisfaction. Lady Darcy had become 'a better lady than ever she was before insomuch that she hath promised me her good ladyship as long as ever she shall live, and if she or ye can find anything meeter for me in these parts or any other, she will help to promote me to the utter most of her puissance [power]'.[23]

HOSPITALITY

Having looked at the lives of the young lady and gentlemen servants in noble households, we shall now turn to the adults. In order to understand the roles of some of them, it is necessary to understand some of the complicated etiquette of Tudor hospitality. The most important point to observe was that guests had to be cared for with a proper regard for their rank and degree. Personal feelings did not enter into the equation. It was also important not to embarrass anyone by placing them with people of a significantly lower social rank. In other words the whole etiquette revolved around reminding everyone involved of their social position.

In order to show due reverence a large household needed both an usher of the chamber and either an usher or marshal of the hall. The job of the marshal of the hall was to keep the hall in order, seeing that it was kept clean, that the fire was attended to, and that furniture for meals was set in place and taken away as necessary. He was also responsible for maintaining order, and ensuring that everyone behaved appropriately. Perhaps the most nerve-wracking part of his job was that of seating people at meals in the hall according to their rank. An usher also had the job of seeing that people were treated according to their rank. Naturally, the usher of the chamber dealt specifically with the room beyond the hall, where only the higher social ranks were allowed to go.[24]

John Russell describes how each rank should be treated. The detail is incredible, as it even included how to treat the pope's foster parents. It is difficult for a modern reader to look at this without laughing, but anyone who actually had to deal with the aristocracy in the fifteenth and sixteenth centuries must have had to know these details by heart. The last thing you wanted to do was upset a powerful visitor, and thus publicly shame your employer, by getting it wrong.

The seating arrangements for meals were only part of the knowledge required. From the moment the arrival of an important visitor was announced, whether they were due or not, the details of the hospitality offered had to be absolutely right.

Men of honour and title had to be met at the gate by senior household officers, even if they appeared unexpectedly during a meal. While meals were in progress the porters who kept the gate were usually required to refuse entry, so this in itself was an honour. The way they were admitted was also of significance. Most visitors would be allowed in through the half-wicket gate, which was much smaller than the main gate and was the usual everyday way in and out for most people. If the visitor's status was as high as that of the owner of the house, or was at least the degree of baron (the lowest level of aristocracy), then such casual manners would not do. The great gateway had to be opened for him, so that he could enter the house in style. If he was of at least the same social status as the owner of the house, he could even claim the right to enter the courtyard on horseback, although even Russell suggests that this was not quite the thing, and should only be done if the head officers really insisted. If the guest was of very exalted rank, and certainly of higher rank than the owner of the house, the social submission of the house's owner had to be shown, so the senior officers of the household would offer him the white staves that were the official emblems of their authority.

The etiquette demanded by no means finished at the door. The guest was escorted through the house, being greeted with due reverence by all the staff. The grander you were, the further you were escorted. A truly exalted guest would not linger in the hall but would be taken directly to the chamber. A lesser visitor would only be escorted to the hall. Some were met at the gate by less important household officers, such as the porter. Such lesser guests were allowed to eat in the hall, but after their meal had to perform their reverence in front of the top table on the dais in the hall to demonstrate their lower social status.

Many people were not even admitted. The free-flowing hospitality that noble houses were famous for was open only to certain people. The poor were not expected even to enter the house unless they were working for the lord in some capacity. Their place was strictly outside the door. This is not to say that they were ignored by the household. It was the job of the wealthy to give alms, so the first slices of meat cut and a loaf were put into a special alms dish before each meal as a reminder to the lord of the house that he must serve God first. Often there was an impressive ceremonial almsdish to take up the alms from the lord's table. Sir John Falstolf had a silver one that weighed an impressive 132oz.[25] The contents of the almsdish and any leftovers were given to the poor, but only after the meal was over. The alms were distributed at the gate, so that the poor were forced to stay at a respectful distance. The person who had the job of overseeing this charity was called the almoner.[26]

Huge numbers of guests passed through great households and must have taken up a great deal of the time not only of the domestic staff but also of the gentlemen employees. George Cavendish gives some idea of the work he had to do as a gentleman usher at the time of the famous visit of the French embassy to Hampton Court, in the years when it was still Wolsey's property rather than a royal palace. This, of course, was an exceptional occasion even by royal standards but it gives an idea of the duties involved in catering for prestigious guests.

At the time of the entertainment Wolsey and his household were actually staying elsewhere, so George and another two gentlemen ushers were sent ahead to check that the palace was ready, that all the rooms had been properly furnished and that all was prepared. They also seem to have had the job of escorting the guests to their chambers and then from their chambers down to the rooms where the feast was held later that evening. George reports a number of tiny details, from the silver plate left in the guests' private quarters for their personal use, to the gifts given to the guests and their attendants as they left. The impression is that a gentleman usher had the job of overseeing every detail of a guest's stay, plus, of course, being his master's eyes and ears to report any gossip or news that might be useful.

The latter point was important as it highlights another issue about gentlemen servants. They were often present on occasions when they could overhear matters concerning their master's private or political life. Knowledge, of course, is power – but it was not always used to the lord's advantage. During the civil wars of the fifteenth century a variety of great men, including the 2nd Duke of Buckingham, were brought down after being betrayed by members of client families who had become servants in their households. A lord needed to choose his gentlemen with care.

ADMINISTRATIVE SERVANTS

A great Tudor lord was a rich man, and his various business interests needed careful attention if he was to maintain his position. He employed a whole team of advisers and managers to help him do this. Before looking at the work that some of these people did, we need to look at what these business interests were as they were far more varied than might be imagined.[27]

Land

Great estates were essential to power. For one thing, they were the most reliable form of investment at the time. They also gave you considerable influence over your tenants and provided you with the manpower you needed. They supplied your household with at least some of the food and fuel it needed. Properly managed, they gave a regular annual income which provided for normal expenditure, such as the wages of your household staff. They could also, on occasion at least, provide you with large sums to pay extraordinary expenses such as the dowry of a daughter. The main problem was to balance all these different needs.

The profits of an estate did not derive simply from the rent received from tenants. Fines, or money due when a lease went to a different person (even if was due to a death in the family, and the old tenant was succeeded by his son), brought in considerable sums. Such fines were also paid when the lord himself died and was replaced by his heir. When Roger Manners, Earl of Rutland, came of age in 1598 he gained something in the region of £14,600[28] from fines as the tenants entered into new leases with him.

There were also other ways of making profits from tenants. They often had obligatory duties written into their contracts, which varied from area to area. The Earl of Northumberland made his tenants cart coal for him at Tynemouth. In 1616 the Earl of Kent gave fifteen-year leases to twelve tenants at Blunham in Bedfordshire and as part of the agreement the tenants had to carry salt fish and other dry goods from Stourbridge fair to any of his lordship's Bedfordshire houses, and also coal from St Ives to Blunham parsonage.[29]

Woods could also be extremely profitable, and were often considered as useful for raising money in an emergency. Trees would be cut down and the timber sold. They could either then be left to grow again, or the cleared land could be used as pasture. Again, the profits could be considerable. Henry, 2nd Earl of Rutland, was advised that he could raise over £6,600 by selling woods in the mid-sixteenth century.[30]

Part of the estate, known as the demesne, was usually kept back to be farmed directly by the lord, rather than being let out to tenants. English landowners seemed reluctant to do this on a large scale, as they always seemed to believe that any profit made would be lost by their servants, who would undoubtedly cheat them. Despite this fear, a great deal of sheep farming was done this way. In the first half of the century this was usually done with a view to producing wool, but after the export boom of wool collapsed in 1551, sheep were raised as much for mutton as for wool as the growing population led to increased demand for meat.

The need to exploit estates more efficiently also led many nobles to get rid of their deer parks. Once the essential status symbol for the great and powerful, many were now turned into pasture and the once-treasured herds of deer driven out to fend for themselves.

Industry

It was not considered suitable for great lords to get too involved in either industry or commerce but that is not to say that they ignored such matters completely. Exploiting the resources of your estate to the maximum was seen as good economics and if this meant activities such as mining or making glass or iron then that was perfectly acceptable. The Earls of Rutland made considerable amounts of money from an ironworks they owned at Rievaulx Abbey. Ironworking had been started there by the monks, but after the property came into the earl's hands after the dissolution, the work continued. As soon as he got permission, the earl began to modernise the works, installing a water-powered hammer in 1540. The earls were very careful managers of the ironworks, taking a great personal interest in both equipping and supplying it. Fuelling the furnaces took a great deal of charcoal, so to avoid the permanent destruction of his woodlands the earl and his agents arranged for the works to be supplied with charcoal from twenty different areas. The idea was to use one area each year, giving each area twenty years to recover before it was used again. The furnace was improved several times. In 1577 the first recorded blast furnace in the north of England was installed and in 1582 an entirely new furnace was added. Improvements went on being made right up until the time of the Civil War.[31] The Earls of Rutland were not alone in showing interest in ironworks either. Robert Dudley, Earl of Leicester, drew £1,600 a year from his ironworks.

Smelting lead was another profitable enterprise. In the 1570s and 1580s the Earl of Shrewsbury was probably the largest lead smelter in the country, with the annual expenses of running one of his works being about £600. Although he was to regret his choice later, his marriage to the celebrated Bess of Hardwick played a part in this as there were lead mines on the land she brought to him as her dowry. He also set up a steelworks to supply the cutlery trade in Sheffield, which was expanding at this time. By the 1590s he was producing between 30 and 45 tons a year, showing a profit of between £200 and £400 annually.[32] Other noblemen exploited salt, alum and building stone from their estates, while others made glass.

Having said that, industry was not yet a way to enormous wealth for most aristocrats. There was only one man, Lord Robartes, who made his wealth through industry (tin in his case) and even he made some of his fortune from money-lending. Ironworks did make money, but they tended to fail once the local fuel supply was used up, a problem which taxed even the resourceful Earls of Rutland. The transport network also remained too poor to allow the easy transport of goods beyond the local area and often the local market was not large enough to support large-scale production. Only in the eighteenth century did industry become the way to enormous wealth.[33] In any case, getting too closely involved with industry could be a mistake among the status-conscious Tudor aristocracy. In the 1560s James, Lord Mountjoy, came in for criticism when he set up house on the site of his alum mine and works at Canford in Dorset, and got involved in the daily chores of the mine manager.

Urban Development

Urban development is certainly not a new phenomenon. The population was expanding in the sixteenth century, and London in particular was a thriving city. If you were fortunate enough to own land in the London area you could become very rich by developing it. It was a way to a much more lasting wealth than industry at this time. After the dissolution much of the land between the city and

Westminster fell into royal hands, but was all soon given away or sold. Those who benefited from this could become very rich indeed. By the end of the sixteenth century Westminster was developing as an administrative centre as the court was based at Whitehall and the law courts at Westminster. London was also developing as a social centre so there was huge demand for housing in just this area.

The Earls of Southampton were very fortunately placed, having inherited an estate in Bloomsbury from the Russells, and also having land to the north of Lincoln's Inn Fields. The earl had begun developing the Lincoln's Inn Fields site by 1594 and by 1638 even went so far as to pull down Southampton House, partly because the outhouses and gardens were already being built over. He was careful to plan the layout and to control the architectural standards to ensure that the area would attract wealthy tenants, so that by the 1640s he was already receiving around £1,000 a year from rents in this area.[34]

Commercial Ventures

The best way of making money from commerce would have been to follow the same paths as the merchants, buying and selling standard commodities over established trade routes. Unfortunately such trading was considered rather beneath an aristocrat. It may well have been too that the aristocracy were looking for more than just commercial return. They loved to gamble by putting their money into voyages of exploration. The Earl of Leicester, for example, backed Drake's circumnavigation of the world and Fenton's attempt to do the same. He also put money into the voyages of Hawkins, Frobisher and Gilbert. George Talbot, Earl of Shrewsbury, invested in Fenton's attempt to reach the East Indies in 1582 and in the Muscovy Company voyage of 1574.

Perhaps investing in such ventures was seen as patriotic. A great number of books on the subject of exploration were published at this time. Richard Hakluyt's much-read *The Principall Navigations, Voiages, Traffiques and Discoveries of the English Nation* certainly puts strong emphasis on the patriotic duty of Englishmen to see that such voyages took place. Quite a few of the aristocracy even owned ships that were offered for such voyages. The Earl of Shrewsbury's *Bark Talbot* went on two commercial voyages to Newfoundland, presumably for cod, but she was also offered to Carleill's colonising expedition to America. However, aristocratic-owned ships were not always used for noble purposes as there was a great deal of money to be made from privateering, especially during the war with Spain, which dragged on between 1585 and 1604.

Privateering was really plain piracy, although when there was a war on you could claim that you were being patriotic in trying to disrupt enemy trade. The Lord Admiral particularly encouraged it as he received 10 per cent of the profits as his due. In the corrupt political climate of the end of Elizabeth's reign courtiers could even maximise their profits by making the crown pick up a large amount of the bill for running a ship, as Robert Cecil's financial affairs demonstrate.

Having been introduced to the joys of privateering by the Lord Admiral, Lord Howard of Effingham, Cecil built a ship with a deceptively romantic name, the *Truelove*. There was certainly nothing romantic about Cecil's attitude to running the ship. He ordered £95 worth of cordage but still hadn't paid for it by 1603, by which time the supplier was in the Fleet prison for debt.

Truelove was sent off privateering in the spring of 1597. By this time Cecil had made sure that she was on the royal payroll, so his expenses were minimal. In June the captain wrote to Cecil telling him of the capture of a Brazilian ship loaded with £1,800-worth of sugar, black slaves and cotton wool. This was sold off in Barbary, while a 120-ton flyboat with a cargo of wine and sugar was sent home to England. Unfortunately the flyboat's owner turned out to be Dutch, which led to complications as England was not at war with Holland.

Cecil was always very careful to spread his capital over a number of voyages, as for him privateering was purely a commercial venture. In 1601–2 his share of the captures made by two ships, *Lioness* and *Refusal*, must have made him about £7,000 profit.[35]

Other aristocratic privateers had different motives, and were not so fortunate. The Earl of Cumberland, a totally different character from Cecil, was a man who craved excitement. He organised no fewer than eleven privateering voyages between 1586 and 1598 and even went to sea in person in six of them. He owned a small fleet of ships and is said to have spent £1,000,000 on his voyages, leading him to speed up the sale of his estates, much to the disgust of his wife.[36]

The economic interests of a great lord could therefore cover a whole variety of different activities, and this does not even take into account the various profits to be had from various court positions. Politics was becoming very corrupt by the end of Elizabeth's reign, and went on to get even worse under James I and Charles I, so the profits of office could be considerable when people were prepared to pay large sums of money to influence political decisions. Given these wide interests, the lord needed a team of talented administrators if his affairs were to prosper.

Having shown some of the sources of aristocratic wealth, it is necessary to point out that sometimes aristocratic duty could also cost you a great deal of money. One of the most expensive duties was to be sent on embassy. While the day-to-day routine diplomatic work would be carried out by an ambassador in residence, high-level embassies also took place. These were usually connected to arranging royal marriages or celebrating the birth of a royal child and the like. At this level only very senior nobles were considered fit for the work. The honour of being chosen for such an embassy was of course considerable, but the cost of it all was so expensive that by the end of Elizabeth's reign people were even risking royal wrath by refusing to go.

The problem was a cross between royal meanness and the increasingly lavish display expected of a diplomat. The crown gave expenses for travel and postage and a salary of £4 to £6 a day. A cash advance of a few hundred pounds was also available. The problem was that this amount never covered the costs involved, and, of course, did not increase as inflation did. The expenses, meanwhile, were enormous. A nobleman had to have the very finest clothes for himself and his attendants. His carriage and horses had to be the very best. He had to entertain lavishly and give suitably impressive gifts to a whole host of people. The basic cost of food and housing was supposed to be met by the host government once he had presented his credentials but there were so many other bills to pay that this didn't make a great deal of difference.

The cost was quite incredible. In the early part of Elizabeth's reign the Earl of Bedford thought that two embassies had left him at least £3,300 out of pocket, which was bad enough. By the end of the reign it was much worse. In 1596 Lord Zouche retired to Guernsey, his fortunes having been shattered by two embassies. The Earls of Northumberland and Rutland and Lords Darcy and Eure all tried to be excused diplomatic duty on the grounds that they couldn't afford it. The embarrassing climax to the problem came in 1603 when Sir William Bowes, ambassador to Scotland, was arrested for debt by a London grocer while on the queen's business.[37] The right royal offices could therefore make you very rich, but the wrong ones could be an enormous financial burden.

ESTATE ADMINISTRATION

Few records of estate administration survive from before the sixteenth century, but by the seventeenth century family records had multiplied, with all sorts of records from private letters to elaborate estate surveys being carefully stored. Some of this expansion could be due to the fact that paper became cheaper and easier to obtain, making it simpler to make records, but much of it was due to the more elaborate records that were needed by the end of the sixteenth century. Sixteenth-century inflation meant that estate owners had to become more efficient and more imaginative in the way they ran their property in order to maintain their income. There was also an enormous growth in litigation around land use. The problem was that there was no centralised land registry, so it was often not clear who owned what land.

The extent of the problem becomes clear when you see how much paperwork was necessary to transfer the ownership of land from one person to another, even when one side was willing to sell and the other to buy. In 1567 the Earl of Leicester bought the manor of Wanstead from Lord Rich. No fewer than seven pieces of parchment were needed to ensure the transfer of ownership. These were: a licence of alienation, a lease and a release, a fine and a recovery, an indenture of bargain and sale and a bond for the performance of covenants. Of course sometimes land changed hands because of a will, the validity of which might be challenged by another member of the family, in which case matters could easily become hugely complicated.

The worst situation was when two powerful families became involved in a dispute and used all their influence to try to get their way. All kinds of skulduggery was indulged in, or at least rumoured to have taken place. John Smyth of Nobley, who wrote a history of Lord Berkeley's family, tells a story of how the Earl of Leicester launched his attempt on part of the Berkeley inheritance in 1570 by getting a herald admitted under false pretences to the Berkeley muniment room, enabling him to steal certain documents vital to the case. In the same way, when there was a big battle over the Dacre inheritance, Lord William Howard of Naworth claimed that his rivals, the Lowers, had stolen documents from the Howard muniment room at the Charterhouse.[38]

Accounting Systems

The accounting systems used by great lords seem so strange to anyone today who has even the most basic knowledge of accounts that it seems amazing to the modern observer that they didn't all go bankrupt. The reason why it seems so odd is that although double-entry bookkeeping was beginning to be used by English merchants, it was still quite unknown among the upper classes. Their accounting systems, based on the 'charge and discharge' method, were not aimed at giving an overall picture of their income and expenditure, but at showing how much each individual financial officer was due to present to his master. The 'charges' were money coming in and the 'discharges' money going out, but they were not arranged in such a way that you knew what your estate produced in a year, and how much it cost to maintain.

As if matters were not confused enough already, no single accountant had overall charge. Different estates had their own financial officers who handled their specific area. Lords often had blocks of estates in different parts of the country. For example, the Rutland accounts for the years 1599–1601 show that there were no fewer than three bailiffs at Belvoir, Helmsley and Garendon, and a clerk of the Rievaulx ironworks. There was a more senior financial officer, the receiver-general, at Belvoir who looked after all the receipts from Lincolnshire, Leicestershire and Nottinghamshire, plus an agent in London and a northern receiver for the Yorkshire estates at Helmsley. There was no central system which brought all these accounts together so there was no record of overall annual profit and loss for the Earl of Rutland's affairs.

The whole situation was further complicated by the fact that many accounts were still being made up in Roman numerals. Doing even simple arithmetic with Roman numerals is much more difficult than with Arabic numerals, so mistakes were not only made more often but were more difficult to detect. Although English was beginning to be used for such records, many were also still made up in Latin, and some went on being in Latin until the middle of the seventeenth century. On top of this, tenants who held farms close to the lord's main seat often paid at least part of the rent in kind, in meat or grain for the lord's kitchen or stables. Such payments often didn't go through the accounts at all.

There were exceptions. The Earls of Salisbury had a far more efficient, centralised system. The Cecils were a 'new' family, with a newly formed estate, so they didn't need to follow the traditional accounting practices of previous ages. Their estates were also not widespread, and so did not require anything but a centralised system. Despite this, in the last years of his life the 2nd Earl was forced to call in an expert to sort out his increasingly chaotic affairs. Some aristocrats' affairs were so complicated that it was difficult to work out exactly what was causing their economic crises. In 1600 Henry, Lord Cobham, called in an expert to sort out his affairs, only to be told that the problem was his wife's extravagance.[39]

THE COUNCIL

In the Middle Ages and early sixteenth century great lords had a council to help them run their business affairs. There was no hard and fast rule as to who sat on this council but it would often consist of the lord's chief officers and some of the leading local gentry. In the 1530s Lord Berkeley's affairs were run by a council which consisted of the steward of the land, an auditor, a receiver and a solicitor, who had the job of visiting each manor annually to collect the rents. The use of the council gradually seems to have fallen out of fashion. By the seventeenth century it was usually only called in to try to sort out difficult situations, such as when the Duke of Buckingham was trying to put right his difficult financial situation in 1622. By the end of the sixteenth century the council was only used regularly when the lord was abroad for some reason and needed someone to take charge in his absence. Viscount Wentworth used his council, which consisted of two of his gentlemen followers, the Revd Charles Green and Sir George Radcliffe, plus his steward and solicitor, to run his lands when he was away in Ireland, working as Lord Deputy.

ADMINISTRATORS

Given the complicated tasks his administrators had to perform, a lord had to choose them with care. The success of the family depended on the quality of the administrators, so it is no surprise that this was an area in which real career progression was possible for a man of talent.

The arrangements a lord made varied according to his own inclinations, how his estates were arranged geographically and, if the family was a long-established one, tradition. Another important factor was where a lord actually chose to live. If, as many of them did, he spent a great deal of time in London then somehow money had to be provided for him there even if his estates were miles from the city.

In terms of personnel, the lowest-ranking financial officer was the bailiff. He collected all the income due to his master from the manor for which he was responsible. This included not only rent but also the income from the manorial court, profits on the sale of woods, etc. He was allowed to deduct expenses for the running of the manor, such as for the upkeep of buildings. A bailiff usually lived on the manor for which he was responsible rather than at the lord's main house. At the top of the ladder was the receiver-general, who collected the money from the bailiffs, the local receivers and any other source. They lived at the lord's main seat, or sometimes even in London. As they were senior servants they would have been entitled to luxuries such as a private room as a matter of course.

The receivers and receivers-general were supervised by auditors, who were usually employed on a part-time basis, since checking the accounts only took about three or four weeks. Thus auditors often worked for a number of different families, moving around as needed. The accounts were usually checked annually but sometimes they were only checked as and when the lord felt like it, as was the case with the Percy accounts.

There also had to be control over the spending of money, as well as collecting it. Various members of the lord's household had to be able to spend on the lord's behalf. The most important of these was the household steward. According to John Russell, the steward was responsible for overseeing the household accounts but sometimes the clerk of the kitchen, who handled considerable sums of money, would deal directly with the receiver-general. The gentlemen of the chamber, who were likely also to be personal friends of the lord, dealt with the lord's personal expenses such as clothes, gambling debts, etc. The gentleman of the horse, who organised transport, was also usually authorised to spend on behalf of his master.

Not all the lord's administrators were concerned with financial matters. There was a large amount of legal work to be done, so the lord always employed a solicitor. There would also be a steward of the courts, who would be responsible for running the manorial courts and entering up the court rolls.

This all sounds very organised and straightforward, but of course in real life everything was much more complicated. Some officers might combine two jobs, for example. However a household's finances were set up, service in this area could provide an excellent career. While personal service declined as a gentlemanly career, lords still needed their finances organised so even in the late sixteenth century (and into the seventeenth) members of the gentry were happy to serve the lord in various financial offices. In 1572 Henry, Earl of Derby, inherited his title and appointed Sir Richard Shireburne of Stonyhurst as treasurer to his household and Edward Scarisbrick as his receiver-general. Both were heads of very prominent local families.

The career possibilities available in the administrative side of great households were genuinely very good. In the early seventeenth century John Southworth progressed from being one of the Earl of Salisbury's gentlemen of the chamber to being his receiver-general just thirteen years later. Allan King, a member of a local gentry family, started out as a bailiff on one of the Earl of Northumberland's manors in 1581, and was steward of the earl's household by 1592. Henry Taylor started his career as the earl's payer of foreign payments, before becoming clerk of the kitchen and ultimately steward of the household.

For the more ambitious, it was also possible to progress into the royal administration. Sir John Daccombe, who was a particularly gifted financial administrator working for the Earl of Salisbury, moved from the earl's household to become chancellor of the Duchy of Lancaster. Some worked for both the aristocracy and the crown. At the beginning of Queen Elizabeth's reign the Duke of Norfolk's agent, William Dix, was also an auditor of the Queen's Prests, advances of money made regarding state business.

The work of many financial officers must have been more interesting than most. Their jobs doubtless brought them a very good standard of living as they would have been treated with a great deal of respect as the representatives of very important men. In other words, their work gave them access to a way of life that they would not have enjoyed had they chosen other career paths. What it didn't necessarily give them was a great deal of money, at least if they remained honest. An example of this is provided by Mr Curuttinden, who was steward to Robert Sydney, Earl of Leicester. He joined Sydney's household as a wardrobe keeper in the 1590s, and after twenty-four years of service he claimed to have built up an estate of £1,000, which was only a fifth of his wife's dowry. He did have more money than this, but it had been built up by trading on his own account in English kerseys and Dutch tobacco rather than directly from his work.

This latter point was important, as not all aristocratic officials used their own money for speculation. Royal servants often purloined any cash in the royal accounts they were responsible for. They would lend it out at interest on their own behalf and take the profits for themselves. When required they would return the original balance, but of course in the meantime the monarch had lost out on the profits the money could have been makng for them. Under the circumstances, it was surprising that aristocratic servants felt free to speculate with any sums of money that their masters left in their care. In 1602 the Earl of Northumberland was informed that his officers were doing just that 'at greate profit to their owne purses'.

A modern observer might wonder why great lords allowed such things to go on, but in fact such ways of making a living were vital. The actual salary an upper servant received, if it existed at all, was usually very low. The Earl of Northumberland's receiver-general was only paid £10 a year at the end of Elizabeth I's reign, while in 1610 the Earl of Huntingdon's clerk of the kitchen was paid just £5 a year. During the seventeenth century salaries for such men rose considerably – the Earl of Northumberland's steward of the household was paid £50 by the 1630s, for example, when he had only been paid £20 in 1598.[40] In the sixteenth century the senior officers of even the greatest men relied on making money in other ways.

William Cecil's household is a good example. As the queen's right-hand man he made a great deal of money out of royal service. As Treasurer he had scores of crown offices at his disposal and as Master of the Wards he could make a great deal of money out of the wardships he controlled. He often passed these rewards on to his servants, in effect as part of their pay. He granted no fewer than fifty-four wardships to thirty-three of his servants. He also used his influence to find positions for the families of favoured servants. Thomas Bellot became Cecil's steward in 1566 and went on working for him for no less than forty years. His brother Owen was appointed the royal woodward in Denbigh and also became steward in a noble family related to the Cecils. John, another brother, was made collector of crown rents in Chester and became steward to the Earl of Rutland, who at one time had been one of Cecil's wards. Still another brother became steward to Sir Raynald Mohun.[41]

Aristocratic service was not necessarily a road to great fortune but you could do reasonably well. George Cavendish, Cardinal Wolsey's gentleman usher, was able to support his wife and children in a manor house, and to leave them a reasonable inheritance.[42] A few people did very well indeed. Sir John Thynne, the builder of Longleat, became extremely wealthy through service as steward to Edward Seymour, later the Duke of Somerset. Not all his wealth derived from his work, however, as he had commercial interests in London and married, as his first wife, the daughter of a wealthy London merchant, Sir Richard Gresham.

Henry Maynard and Michael Hickes, both secretaries to Cecil, became rich through their service and also used the money they made for lending at interest. Maynard left the vast sum of £4,500 in cash. His eldest son became a baron, the second a leading courtier and the third Auditor of the Exchequer. Hickes's son William became a baronet, probably by purchase. Both doubtless earned their money from Cecil. But although he was known for rewarding his staff well, Cecil also made them work as hard as he did himself.[43]

FRIENDSHIP

A nobleman's personal servants were his constant companions, and a sensible man chose them with care. Henry Percy, 9th Earl of Northumberland, who succeeded his father in 1585 at the age of twenty-one, learnt the importance of this the hard way. He blames his mistakes partly on his upbringing, through the 'ignorance fostered in me by my father's concealing of that was fit for me to have been made acquainted withal'. As a result he chose personal servants who wanted to hunt, gamble, dally with mistresses and spend money on clothing just as he did – and he ended up heavily in debt as a result. He wrote this down in his *Advice to His Son*, hoping to persuade the boy to choose with more care. This incident demonstrates very effectively the importance of friendship between a nobleman and his personal attendants.[44]

Michael Hickes became a close personal friend of William Cecil's son Robert while working in the Cecil household, which was one important reason why his career continued to prosper after William Cecil's death in 1598. This shows another vital function of the senior officers of the household of any great man, in that they were often companions who not only worked for him but also hunted with him and generally shared his social life. Friendship is obviously difficult to quantify, but there does often seem to have been a close bond between such men which went deeper than the self-interest of those involved. Michael Hickes was with Robert Cecil when he died, having attended him to Bath where he was receiving medical treatment. As Hickes was almost seventy at the time this must have been no small effort for him. The last letter that survives from Hickes is also full of concern at his friend's health. Even at the highest levels friendship could sometimes outweigh self-interest. Several of Anne of Cleves's ladies were so attached to her that they chose to remain in her service even when she was no longer queen, rather than staying on to work for the new queen, Katherine Howard.

At a lower level George Cavendish would not have presumed to make a personal friend of so great a man as Cardinal Wolsey but he clearly retained some affection for him, writing his *Life and Death of Cardinal Wolsey* at least twenty years after Wolsey's death. He also refused a place in the royal household after Wolsey's death and retired, disillusioned, to the country.[45]

This personal note brings home a very important point about service for the rich and powerful in the sixteenth century. Even financial officers and administrators were resident in the household with the lord at least occasionally, while servants involved with hospitality lived there all the time. This meant that to do well in any of these forms of service you had to be able to socialise effectively with the lord and your peers. This was why there was such an enormous emphasis on bringing up gently bred children to be agreeable in society. The ability to make witty or at least interesting conversation, to join in music and dancing or the hunt was vital to success. The rounded education given to gently bred children clearly fitted them well for the world in which they lived and worked when they grew up.

SEVEN

Stars in the Presence of the Sun
Personal Servants to Royalty

In some respects the royal household was very like that of any great lord, only bigger and grander. Like other households, it was divided into the service section and the section designed for the personal service of the lord and master. However, in this case the lord and master was the monarch, meaning that personal service and politics were closely linked. At this time, if you had access to the monarch and enjoyed their favour, then all sorts of interesting and profitable opportunities were open to you. This was why personal service to the monarch was so highly sought after.

THE LAYOUT OF THE ROYAL APARTMENTS

Before considering what life was like in the royal apartments, you need to understand how they were arranged. For reasons we shall look at later, the layout of the rooms changed as the sixteenth century progressed, and not all palaces were the same in any case. The largest palaces, where full court was kept, had whole suites of royal apartments, while the smaller, less formal ones had more modest arrangements. The royal apartments at Henry VIII's palace at Nonsuch, for example, really only had a bedchamber and a couple of small private rooms, known as closets. Even so, despite the changes, the general principle remained the same. While the rooms intended for public display were large, the private rooms in which the monarch actually lived were small and intimate. For this reason, the further into the royal apartments you went, the smaller the rooms tended to become.[1]

At the end of the fifteenth century, when Henry VII was on the throne, royal apartments were not particularly extensive. Previous kings had had a guard or great chamber, a presence chamber in which they dined in state and received important visitors, and finally a privy chamber which was a private bedroom and sitting room. As we shall see later, Henry VII was particularly keen to keep his privy chamber private, and access to it was very carefully guarded indeed.

By Henry VIII's time things were changing. A fashion for more privacy was spreading across Europe, and Henry was a man to whom fashion was important. The royal private apartments developed into more the kind of accommodation we might expect royalty to enjoy today. Henry was the greatest royal builder ever to have ruled England, and he certainly didn't stint on his private rooms. The extension to the royal apartments he began building at Hampton Court in 1529 was three storeys high and contained an office at ground-floor level, a new bedroom, bathroom and study on the first floor and a library and jewel house on the second floor. At Whitehall in 1531 he started to build a new privy lodging, conveniently laid out on one level on the first floor, except for the bathroom, which was on the ground floor. The first floor provided at least ten rooms for the king.

As the royal apartments grew, so some of the rooms changed their use. The privy chamber, once a very private room indeed, now became more and more public, until most of the senior members of the court had access to it. It then became a public room to such an extent that ennoblements, which at one time took place in the presence chamber, now moved into it. In 1542, for example, Sir John Dudley became Viscount Lisle in the privy chamber at Whitehall.

As if that were not enough, the royal apartments became open to other groups of courtiers. The Privy Council, which formally came into existence in 1540, met in council chambers within the private apartments. This brought another group of courtiers into the royal private space, which was now in danger of becoming not very private at all. It was no surprise that the royal private rooms multiplied as Henry tried to keep some rooms genuinely private. As we shall see, access to the truly private rooms was very jealously guarded. You could judge a courtier's status by the rooms he was allowed to enter.

The decoration and furnishing of the royal rooms would surprise us now. Modern interior design tends to focus on furniture, but in the sixteenth century there was more of a focus on textiles, especially wall-hangings of various kinds. This was quite logical given that great households, noble and royal alike, were only just beginning to become more static after centuries of living on the move. Henry VIII travelled far less than medieval kings had done, but still his court moved about thirty times a year. Textiles are obviously more easily moved than furniture. From the mid-sixteenth century rich furniture does become more common, but Tudor royal apartments would seem sparsely furnished by our standards. Even the great and the good could find themselves perched on windowsills or chests, or even sitting on a cushion on the floor, as the picture of Elizabeth I receiving Dutch ambassadors shows (see plate 1 of colour plates).

Just as there was a careful hierarchy of rooms, so there was a hierarchy of decoration. The most prestigious rooms were adorned with gold, preferably solid gold, and hung with best-quality cloth of gold. The effect of such decoration must have been stunning when rooms were lit by candles and heated by fires, when the light would play on the gold. After gold came not silver but the best quality tapestries, which would often have gold and silver threads woven into them. Next came silver decoration, then the various grades of lesser tapestries, using expensive fabrics such as velvets and silks, and embroideries. Paintings came at the bottom of the scale. This hierarchy of decoration was used very carefully in important public rooms. A good example comes from the preparations for the marriage in 1508 of Henry VII's sister Mary to Charles, Prince of Castille. Like many projected royal marriages, this one never took place, but a list of Princess Mary's requirements still exists, annotated, it is thought, by no less a person than Henry VII himself.

The list includes a number of items, ranging from horses and their equipment to jewels and plate, which it was considered necessary for Princess Mary to take with her to Spain on her marriage. The most important section from our point of view was the list of fabrics and furnishings necessary for her apartments, which were evidently to consist of four rooms. The first and most important room was her bedchamber, which was to be hung with cloth of gold, with a border embroidered with her heraldic badges. It was to be furnished with a chair upholstered in cloth of gold. The bed was to have a celor, tester and bedcover of the same cloth of gold, while the curtains were to be of damask. The second room was to be hung with 'a riche story of Aras gold and silke of iiij yerdes depe, with a border of her armys and bagies for a remembraunce', with gold and purple velvet furnishings. The third room was to be hung with tapestry without gold and silver threads and the upholstery was to be velvet, although the bedspread was to be of velvet and cloth of gold. The fourth and final room was simply to be decorated with good tapestry.[2]

Not all the rooms in the royal apartments were decorated with such symbolism in mind. Private rooms of lesser political significance were decorated more with a view to comfort and pleasing the eye. The walls were often panelled or wainscoted (that is, panelled to about two-thirds of the height of the room). The panelling was often painted or even gilded. If not panelled, the walls could be plastered and painted. A number of murals are known to have existed in the royal palaces, including one of Adam and Eve and another famous one of Henry VIII and Jane Seymour, with Henry's parents standing behind them. Both were at Whitehall. Elaborate plasterwork, either as friezes or ceilings, was also often used. Certainly you wouldn't find bare brick or stone, as neither was admired inside buildings in the sixteenth century.

WORKING IN THE ROYAL APARTMENTS

Given that the job of the royal personal servants was to make the private life of the monarch as comfortable as possible, the exact nature of the work was bound to change as kings and queens came and went. A great deal has been written over the years about how the different Tudor monarchs used their private staff, who can most easily be described as those who staffed the privy chamber, the chamber which was originally the monarch's private space. Before considering what it was like working for the Tudor monarchs you need some understanding as to how the job of the privy chamber staff changed over time.

Henry VII is often overlooked. He never seems to later generations to have had the glamour of either his son Henry VIII or his granddaughter Elizabeth I. This was because he was a person who valued his privacy – and for a very good reason. Henry, whose claim to the throne was not very strong, had managed not only to fight his way to the throne but to keep it. A very clever politician, he had learnt the hard way that the fewer people he trusted, the better. In 1495, ten years after he had fought his way to the throne, Henry's step-uncle Sir William Stanley, who held the post of Lord Chamberlain, was found guilty of treasonable communication with Perkin Warbeck. The Lord Steward, John, Lord Fitzwalter, was also implicated. No wonder Henry wanted a private place to work in, attended only by a small staff of trusted men.[3]

Henry decided to make the privy chamber even more private by providing it with its own special staff. The more formal section of the royal apartments, often known as the chamber, was run by the Lord Chamberlain, who was a peer, and by a staff of hundreds. The privy chamber had only six grooms, who were supervised by the groom of the stool. None of the privy chamber staff were peers; in fact, the groom of the stool was a mere gentleman and some of those beneath him not even that. Hugh Denys, who was groom of the stool for most of Henry VII's reign, came from a well-established Gloucestershire gentry family but was certainly no magnate.[4] This was, of course, all part of the idea. Great lords were more likely to have their own agenda than lesser men, who would understand that their loyalties lay with the king. Henry VII did not want any political factions developing in his private space.

Another great advantage to Henry VII's mind was that by keeping the number of staff small and employing only men of lower status, ceremony could be kept out of the privy chamber. Henry VII was a very hard-working king who kept a very close eye on the details of government. He also realised the value of playing his cards close to his chest, so that even his councillors did not know what his intentions were, but were merely expected to carry out the royal wishes. It was therefore understandable that he didn't want all the elaborate ceremonial of royal public life in the room where he worked.

Having said all this, the staff of the privy chamber did not work only in the quiet confines of the court. They were trusted royal servants, and so were useful for diplomatic missions. They could also be sent off around the country to represent the king in places where he could not go himself, so their lives were not spent entirely in the royal presence. Francis Marzen, one of the grooms of the privy chamber, served as a diplomat on several occasions and was even knighted in 1506.[5]

Henry VIII was such a different personality from his father that life in the royal privy chamber was bound to change considerably when he came to the throne. He felt no need to maintain a dignified distance from the court as his father had done; in fact, quite the reverse. Henry was a young man of nearly eighteen when he came to the throne, well aware of his good looks and intending to shine on both the national and international level. He certainly had no intention of locking himself away in private for most of the day reading state papers. He also wanted to surround himself with his friends, which gave him a problem. There simply weren't enough high-status jobs in the privy chamber. The groom of the stool was a good job, as the senior royal body servant, responsible for the king's everyday jewels and plate and also performing some important administrative duties. The other jobs were not really of the sort that a man of high status could be expected to do. Henry did appoint one of his friends, Nicholas Carew, as a groom of the privy chamber, but he was very young at the time and only did the job for a year.

The answer to the problem came, as it so often did in Henry VIII's time, by copying the French court. Francis I, who was even younger than Henry, came to the French throne in 1515, and Henry spent a great deal of his reign competing with Francis. This was not always an easy thing to do, as in the sixteenth century France was a more powerful country than England. However, in this case the French model was not so difficult to follow.

Francis had decided that he too wished to be attended by men of standing, for whom the traditional post of valet de chamber simply would not do. His answer was to create the post of gentilhomme de la chambre. The post came to England quite naturally in 1518, as at that time Henry was working on developing more peaceful relations with France. A French embassy came to England, and etiquette demanded that there be English versions of the gentilhommes de la chambre to pair with their French counterparts. Of course, the title in England soon became gentleman rather than gentilhomme. The gentlemen did, of course, help the king dress, serve his dinner and generally keep him entertained when he required company, but that was only the beginning of their duties. An effective gentleman needed to be the fashionable Renaissance courtier, skilled in many different areas of government.

The gentlemen of the privy chamber were to prove very useful, especially as the two most influential courts in Europe at the time, those of Francis I and Charles V, organised their monarch's personal service much as Henry VIII did his. This meant that the courts could exchange gentlemen for diplomatic purposes, and they could work in the foreign monarch's private apartments much as they did when at home. This must have been quite a tall order when international relations were frosty, as was often the case between England and France. No wonder social skills were so much part of a would-be courtier's education. The Eltham Ordinances state that the king's gentlemen should be 'well languaged, experte in outward parts, and meete and able to be sent on familiar messages'.[6] In other words, they needed not only linguistic skills but also elegant social skills and the right qualities to make them able to convey the more delicate messages that kings had to exchange as privately as they could in the days before telephones existed. An ability to fit in was certainly required, and many of them did that extremely well. A portrait of Anthony Browne, painted either during or soon after an extended stay in France in 1518–19, shows him to be the very image of a Frenchman.[7]

A man of rank at this time underwent military training as a matter of course, so the gentlemen of the privy chamber (and indeed the other members of the privy chamber) were frequently involved in military matters of various kinds. As men of standing, they could often raise quite considerable military forces to fight for the king. William Compton, for example, led no fewer than 578 men during Henry's invasion of France in 1513.[8]

Some had rather more exotic roles. Sir Peter Mewtis, an acknowledged expert in handguns, was sent abroad in 1537 with the aim of killing Cardinal Pole with a handgun. In 1546 he was sent to Normandy as a spy, his French being so perfect that he was assumed to be a native.[9]

The privy chamber staff were also vital in helping the king run the country, at both a local and a national level. The fact that they lived and worked so closely with the king gave them extra authority in the eyes of those they dealt with, so they were ideal people to represent the monarch. At a local level members of the privy chamber held a variety of posts. George, Viscount Rochford, and Sir Thomas Cheyney, both gentlemen of the privy chamber, held the wardenship of the Cinque Ports at different times, while John, Lord Russell, was president of the Council of the West. They weren't always particularly good at their work. Compton, who was Sheriff of Worcestershire, was both oppressive and greedy but the important point as far as Henry VIII was concerned was that such men were very loyal to the crown.[10]

Henry VIII's body servants therefore had considerable political power, which they exercised not only through the offices they held but also through their ability to persuade the king to sign documents. This was no small point. Ministers and their administrative teams drafted legislation, but however carefully they did their work no document carried the force of law until it had been signed by the king. Henry was never interested in the details of government, which he left to servants such as Wolsey and Cromwell. He had always hated writing, but as he got older and his health declined he developed a real dislike of even signing his name. In the end the sign manual had to be used. This was a metal stamp which imprinted the king's signature at the bottom of a document. The impression was then inked over by a clerk. This, of course, had the potential of giving the chamber staff even more power.[11]

Another factor which complicated the politics of the privy chamber was the fact that Henry was remarkably open to persuasion. The image in the royal portraits might be of a resolute, determined monarch who made up his own mind, but the reality was different. There was a constant struggle between ministers and individuals, and between different factions, for the king's support, which could swing from one group to another. This meant that even very powerful men, such as Cardinal Wolsey, could find their plans ruined by the privy chamber staff who spent large amounts of time with Henry, and who were therefore often able to persuade him to do what they wanted.

This faction fighting can be demonstrated by the relatively unimportant case of Mrs Vernon's marriage in 1517. Mrs Vernon was a wealthy widow whom Wolsey intended as a prize for one of his supporters. In the end she married William Coffin, one of Henry's younger friends, who was helped by Nicholas Carew, another great friend of the king who used his influence to sway him. Wolsey was much annoyed, and managed to get most of this group packed off to Calais in May 1519. By October 1519, though, they were all back at court, and Wolsey was only able to get rid of them again in 1525, when he managed to persuade the king to agree to major reforms of the staffing of the privy chamber in the Eltham Ordinances.[12]

Some small hint of this power struggle can be found in the Eltham Ordinances, wherein the staff of the king's private apartments are warned that none 'shall advance himselfe further in service, than by the King's highnesse he shall be appointed unto; nor presse his Grace in making of sutes, nor intermeddling of causes or matters whatsoever they be'.[13] Of course this had absolutely no effect whatsoever as the fundamental reason for wanting a job in the private apartments was to 'intermeddle'. In any case no minister, not even Wolsey or Cromwell, was able to destroy the influence of the privy chamber staff. It continued to be a hotbed of political scheming well beyond Henry VIII's death and on into Edward VI's reign.

If you wanted to pursue a career in Henry VIII's privy chamber it was vital to be a good politician. If you got it wrong, the results could be fatal, and even some men who at one time stood very high in the royal favour ended up on the block. Henry Courtenay, Marquess of Exeter, was just such a person. He was brought up with Henry and was a close friend for many years, but he was executed when Thomas Cromwell, who saw him as a dangerous rival, turned the king against him. Nicholas Carew, another long-standing friend of the king, was also executed despite his long service. The politics of the privy chamber did not end when Henry VIII died. Edward VI was far from being a mere puppet, despite his young age. The chronicle he made of his reign shows that he was no fool, and he certainly had a mind of his own. However, his reign was of course very short, and he died before his political majority, so most of the political manoeuvring centred around who exactly controlled the young king.

The greatest change to life in the royal apartments came when the king was replaced with a queen. A female monarch had to be attended by women rather than men. In an age when women simply did not hold political office, this made a huge difference to the practicalities of working as one of the monarch's personal attendants. The privy chamber became far more domestic and centred more on providing comfort and companionship for the queen than on political manoeuvring.

The personalities of both Mary and Elizabeth were also important in bringing about this change. Even those female attendants who weren't married still had brothers, uncles, fathers and other family members whose cause they represented, so political wrangling could in theory have been just as much a part of life in the royal privy chamber as it had been when there was a king on the throne. However, both Mary and Elizabeth were far less susceptible to outside pressure than their father had been. Elizabeth in particular made it very clear indeed to her ladies that she did not expect them to try to influence her decisions in political matters, and any attempts to influence her choice of potential husbands was quickly squashed. Even Elizabeth's beloved Catherine Asteley was taught in no uncertain terms not to meddle in politics in this way. She and Dorothy Bradbelte were put under house arrest for writing to the King of Sweden concerning the queen's marriage without permission. Although both returned to their positions the following month, Elizabeth had made her point.[14]

Even before this incident the fact that the queen wished to keep politics out of her private apartments had been noted. The Spanish ambassador De Feria wrote at the beginning of the reign that the queen had resolved not to discuss business with her ladies. At the end of the reign Sir Robert Cross wrote to Robert Cecil: 'Your speech to me in your chamber at Nonsuch some three years past was that I depended and was at charge with women to solicit for me and that the queen would give them good words yet they should never effect suit. I have found that to be true advice.'[15]

You can understand why a queen would want to keep politics out of the privy chamber as much as possible. It was extremely tough being a female monarch in a male world, and a place to relax must have been vital. Mary's marriage never really worked and Elizabeth never married, so what both wanted from their ladies was emotional support as far removed from politics as it was possible to be at court.

THE WORK OF THE ROYAL ATTENDANT

The number of strange-sounding posts, such as groom of the stool or even lady-in-waiting, makes royal life seem either romantic or extremely odd depending on your view of such things. In fact most of the work they did while in attendance was the same as that done by any lady or gentleman attendant working for a great lord or lady.

The Men

The groom of the stool, or stole, is probably the best known of the royal personal servants, not least because his title derives from the close stool or toilet. He did indeed attend his master when he went to the toilet but this was the least of his duties. The groom of the stool was the most important royal body servant. He waited on the king from the moment he got up to when he went to bed. He was also in charge of the king's private apartments, supervising its staff and also having care of the plate and jewels that the king used every day. He also had various administrative duties, although these changed in the ebb and flow of the politics of the privy chamber. For example, at one time the groom was the keeper of Henry VIII's sign manual. As he was the principal private attendant, he also performed the more discreet services required by the king. William Compton, Henry's groom of the stool early in his reign, arranged on at least one occasion for the king to meet a mistress.

Under the groom of the stool came the gentlemen of the privy chamber. In 1525, when the Eltham Ordinances were drawn up, there were six gentlemen but in practice the numbers varied and were usually higher. Their job at its most basic was to wait on the king. The Eltham Ordinances state that two of them were to sleep on a pallet in the privy chamber every night.[16] This would be partly a security measure and partly in case the king should want them for any reason in the night. As we have seen, though, their job also included everything from leadership in times of war to diplomatic missions. It is also important to remember that this job, and that of the groom of the stool, usually went to men who were the king's personal friends. These men spent huge amounts of time with the king and it was only natural that he would employ people he liked in such posts.

At this point it is worth mentioning the esquires of the body. In Henry VII's time these were the principal personal servants of the king.

The Articles for the Regulations of Henry VII's household said that the esquires of the body 'and noe man else to sett hand on the King'[17] as they were the men who helped the king dress. In Henry VIII's time the title of gentlemen of the privy chamber was developed (see above) and they took over in importance from the esquires. Wolsey, who feared the influence that the gentlemen had over the king, tried to get rid of them and to revive the esquires, but despite a temporary victory through the Eltham Ordinances, he ultimately failed and the title esquire of the body gradually faded away.

After the gentlemen came the grooms. A groom at this time was a trained servant and was not necessarily connected with horses. The grooms of the privy chamber were responsible for the rooms they worked in at a more basic level. It was the grooms who cleaned the rooms, moved furniture, and carried torches, etc.

In 1525 two gentlemen ushers were included among the privy chamber staff. The job of ushers generally was to make sure that only the right people were allowed in places of restricted access. This inevitably meant that sometimes they had to refuse access to people who felt affronted by this denial. This could sometimes make them unpopular, as the affair of Simon Bowyer, gentleman usher of the privy chamber to Elizabeth I shows. A well-respected figure at court, Bowyer was in the queen's favour. She told him to turn away from the privy chamber all those whose credentials were insufficient to allow them entry. In following these orders Bowyer turned away a client of the queen's favourite, Robert Dudley, Earl of Leicester. The earl was furious that a client of his should be treated like this, and it was Bowyer on whom his anger fell, since even Leicester had the sense not to take it out on the queen. Throughout the conflict Elizabeth took Bowyer's side, not least because she wanted to make the point that no courtier, however powerful, had the right to control access to the throne.[18] Bowyer was, in fact, only doing his job but it made him a powerful enemy at court, despite the queen's support.

The most junior member of the privy chamber staff was the page. The Eltham Ordinances state that the page was to be in continual attendance.[19] He would be a young gentleman who was there to do whatever the king asked, such as run errands or take messages. Such a position would be a wonderful entrée into the world of the court for some well-connected young man. In fact, this was such a good educational opportunity that the king's counsellors, the chamberlains of both the king and queen, the vice-chamberlains, the Captain of the Guard, the Master of Horse, the henchmen and the gentlemen of the privy chamber were all allowed to have one page each, 'to the intent that young gentlemen may be brought up in service and nurture'.[20]

The gentlemen pensioners are also worth including here as they are often mentioned in connection with the privy chamber. They were set up by Cromwell in 1539–40 as a body of very well-equipped soldiers who acted as a royal bodyguard. As their name suggests, they were gentlemen, and had an impressive uniform which included a gold chain and a gilt poleaxe. At court they stood in the presence chamber, guarding the way to the privy chamber although their captain, Sir Anthony Browne, was a senior gentleman of the privy chamber.[21]

The Ladies

In his *Chronicle of the Kings of England* (1643), Richard Baker describes Elizabeth I:

> Never Prince kept greater State with lesse statelinesse, her Pensioners and Guard were always the tallest and goodliest Gentlemen and Yeomen of the Kingdom, her maids of Honour and other women about her, the fairest and most beautifull Ladies of the Realm, and yet her self a Diana amongst her Nymphes, insomuch that a great Lord of France being entertained at Court, and the Queen asking him how he liked her Ladies made answer, It was hard to judge of Stars, in presence of the Sun.[22]

This passage describes rather delightfully the job of a lady attendant. She had to look good, to behave elegantly and to entertain her mistress, but never, never to outshine her.

Elizabeth I receiving the Dutch ambassadors. Note the lack of furniture, so that her ladies sit on cushions. *(By permission of Staatliche Museen Kassel)*

A black trumpeter on the Westminster Tournament Roll. He is likely to be John Blank. *(By permission of The College of Arms, London)*

Left: The splendours of dining in a great house. This silver gilt pillar salt was really a table decoration rather than a salt cellar and was a dramatic way of demonstrating who was sitting 'above the salt'. *(By permission of the British Museum)*

Right: Livery badges such as these were worn by those in the pay of great families to demonstrate their allegiance. This one shows the arms of the Gainsford family of Surrey and dates between 1525 and 1550. *(By permission of Earl Compton/British Museum)*

Below: Burghley House, one of the houses built by William Cecil. *(By permission of Burghley House)*

Lower servants and others relaxing at the Field of Cloth of Gold. The fountain ran with wine, rather than water, which explains some of the interesting behaviour. *(Detail from* The Field of the Cloth of Gold*/DB/The Royal Collection © 2005 Her Majesty Queen Elizabeth II)*

Mary Fitton, by an unknown artist. She lost her place as a maid of honour when she fell pregnant by the Earl of Pembroke, who refused to marry her. *(By permission of The Viscount Daventry)*

Sir Nicholas Carew, by Hans Holbein. His one-time friendship with Henry VIII did not prevent his execution when he fell out of favour. *(Collection of The Duke of Buccleuch & Queensberry, KT)*

Opposite: Henry VIII reading in his bedchamber in 1540, from *Henry VIII's Psalter*. This seems to be an imaginary setting, but gives a feel for the splendour of the royal private apartments. *(Bridgeman Art Library/Roy 2 A XVI f. 3 © The British Library)*

BEATVS vir qui non abiit
in conſilio impiorum, & in via
peccatorum non ſtetit, & in cathedra pe=
ſtilentiæ non ſedit.

George Gisze, a wealthy merchant, by Holbein. The Turkey carpet on the table and the silver timepiece placed on it demonstrate his wealth. *(Bridgeman Art Library/ Gemaldegalerie, Berlin)*

The opportunities available for ladies at court varied a little depending on whether the monarch was male or female. There was a little more scope for those ladies attending queens regnant rather than queen consorts. Throughout the sixteenth century there were three basic jobs available: lady-in-waiting, maid of honour and chamberer. Ladies-in-waiting were usually married while the maids were young unmarried girls, although sometimes single women moved up from being maids of honour to more responsible posts, especially in the time of Elizabeth I. Chamberers were untitled women who were responsible for the practical running of the royal apartments, taking charge of the queen's linen (bed linen rather than underwear), water bowls, locks and keys and other domestic items.[23] There were not very many posts available at any level. In Elizabeth I's household there were, on average, four ladies of the bedchamber (see below), eight gentlewomen of the privy chamber, six maids of honour and four chamberers.[24] Of course, if there was no queen, as was the case for over two years after the death of Jane Seymour, there were no official posts at court for ladies.

Queen consorts had less say as to the choice of their attendants than queens regnant. The king had the final say in the matter, and there were many ladies who were simply too important to ignore. Catherine of Aragon's ladies-in-waiting came from the very highest rung of society and included the Duke of Buckingham's sisters Elizabeth and Anne Stafford, and Margaret Pole, all of whom were descendants of Edward IV. In practice such ladies did not usually attend the queen on a daily basis, but only on formal occasions when the full weight of courtly magnificence was felt necessary. The everyday attendance on the queen was carried out by ladies of the privy chamber, who were not quite so exalted but were still exceedingly grand. In the case of Catherine of Aragon's staff, these included ladies from families such as the Talbots, Greys and Howards. They had all married into the baronage, except for Lady Boleyn. She was a Howard but had married the relatively humble Sir Thomas Boleyn.[25]

Those ladies who attended a queen consort also had to remember where their loyalties lay. Their obedience was due not to their mistress but to the king. The brave ladies who stood by Catherine of Aragon after she had been rejected by the king shared with their mistress the royal wrath. Those ladies foolish enough to ignore Katherine Howard's infidelities instead of reporting them were to find that forgetting their duty to the king was a serious mistake. Ladies as various as the dowager Duchess of Norfolk and Lady Bridgewater and the less exalted Katherine Tylney were sentenced to perpetual imprisonment and forfeiture of their goods for this crime, although in practice most were eventually pardoned and released. Not all were so lucky. Lady Rochford, who had actually helped Katherine meet her lover, paid for her mistakes with her life, being executed at the same time as her mistress.

Attending a queen regnant was slightly different, although neither Mary nor Elizabeth changed the basic structure of the royal household. Elizabeth simply made the Queen's Side of the royal household larger while reducing the King's Side to a ceremonial Lord's Side, which was presided over by whichever leading nobleman happened to be in court at the time.[26] Her four senior ladies now became known as ladies of the bedchamber. Elizabeth also had no direct equivalent of the groom of the stool, but appears to have divided up the job between the four ladies of the bedchamber. Catherine Asteley seems to have inherited the job of attending the queen at her close stool, as she became the keeper of the royal close stools.

Not all the ladies in attendance on the queen were constantly at court and not all were paid. There were six ladies of high social rank who were listed as members of the privy chamber at the beginning of the reign. They, like Catherine of Aragon's most elevated ladies, served only on the most formal of occasions. Another group served only 'when the queen's Majesty calleth for them'. They may have been 'on call' to serve when other ladies were unavailable for some reason, such as illness. Some of these unsalaried ladies eventually won salaried jobs in the privy chamber, though a degree of patience might be needed. At Elizabeth's accession Dorothy, Lady Edmunds, was appointed extraordinary gentlewoman of the privy chamber but it was 1570 before she succeeded to a salaried post.[27]

The royal ladies, whether they attended a queen regnant or queen consort, obviously had no political or administrative duties but some did have jobs that involved a large amount of responsibility at a domestic level. Looking after the queen's personal jewels and certain furnishings and equipment in the royal apartments was one such role. The other was mistress of the robes, who took responsibility for receiving large amounts of fabric or completed garments, which could be worth a large amount of money. She also had to see that everything required was in the right place at the right time, as some items were stored at the Tower while others might be sent out to the tailors for alterations or repairs. Given the complexity of sixteenth-century dressing, this was no small responsibility. Even so, the career prospects for such ladies were very meagre compared to the many possibilities open to the men attending a king.

Of course, queens did not only employ women in their households. While those who performed intimate services obviously had to be women, it should be remembered that there were still men working in the privy apartments. Simon Bowyer, the gentlemen usher who so annoyed Robert Dudley, was an example.

Splendour and Display

Another important part of the job of royal attendants, both male and female, was display. We have touched on this already, with the description of Elizabeth's ladies as playing the stars to Elizabeth's sun. Today this part of a royal attendant's job sounds rather unimportant but the Tudors well understood the value of display. Royalty expected to dazzle and impress in the days when the display you put on was seen as a sign of your political power. This was why diplomats often wrote home giving details of royal entertainments, outfits worn and gifts given. The ladies and gentlemen in attendance were expected to play their part in putting on a good show.

Henry VIII's passion for hunting caused a problem in this regard. He spent so much time out hunting that the court all tried to follow him, perhaps in the hope of catching the king at a quiet moment to place a petition. The result was not only that the hunt was spoilt, with the animals being scared away by so many hunt followers, but also that 'the court hath been left disgarnished'.[28] The reason why this 'disgarnishing' was such a problem was that it was considered important that the royal houses should be full of people during the hours when the court was open for business. Arriving to find the court half-empty not only disappointed visitors but also suggested to them that the court was not worth visiting, thus destroying the status of the court that royalty took such care to maintain.

The other obvious use of ladies and gentlemen in court display came during the famous court entertainments, but there was also a great deal of daily ceremony, at least when the monarch was holding full court at one of the larger palaces. Paul Hentzner, a German who was touring Europe as tutor to a noble, came to Elizabeth I's court and described what he saw there. One thing that impressed him was the elaborate ritual that surrounded the serving of the royal dinner:

> A Gentleman entered the room bearing a rod, and along with him another who had a table-cloth, which after they had both kneeled three times, with thc utmost veneration, he spread upon the table, and after kneeling again, they both retired. Then came two others, one with the rod again, the other with a salt-seller, a plate, and bread; when they had kneeled, as the other had done, and placed what was brought upon the table, they too retired with the same ceremonies performed by the first. At last came an unmarried Lady (we were told she was a Countess) and along with her a married one, bearing a tasting-knife; the former was dressed in white silk, who when she had prostrated herself three times, in the most graceful manner approached the table and rubbed the plates with bread and salt, with as much awe, as if the Queen had been present: When they had waited there a little while, the Yeomen of the Guard entered, bare-headed, cloathed in scarlet, with a golden rose upon their backs, bringing in at each turn a course of twenty-four dishes, served in plate most of it gilt; these dishes were received by a Gentleman in the same order they were brought,

> and placed upon the table, while the Lady-Taster gave to each of the guard a mouthful to eat, of the particular dish he brought, for fear of any poison. During the time that this guard, which consists of the tallest and stoutest men that can be found in all England, being carefully selected for this service, were bringing dinner, twelve trumpets, and two kettle-drums made the hall ring for half an hour together. At the end of this ceremonial, a number of unmarried Ladies appeared, who with particular solemnity lifted the meat off the table, and conveyed it to the Queen's inner and more private chamber, where after she had chosen for herself, the rest goes to the Ladies of the Court.[29]

Meanwhile, Elizabeth kept herself at a distance, perhaps also enjoying the peace and quiet of as private a meal as a queen ever got, as Hentzner continues: 'The Queen dines and sups alone with very few attendance; and it is very seldom that any body, foreigner or native, is admitted at that time, and then only at the intercession of somebody in power.' This piece of theatre was made all the more powerful by the fact that the queen herself never appeared.

The grace of the ladies and the height and strength of the yeomen were not a matter of chance. Good looks were important if you wanted to make a career at court. Lady Mary Sidney (mother of Sir Philip) was a victim of this need to look good. In 1562 Elizabeth nearly died of smallpox. Part of the job of her ladies was to nurse the queen at such times, and Lady Mary, who was close to Elizabeth, did so with such devotion that she caught the disease herself. She recovered, but the disease left her severely disfigured. Her husband Sir Henry sadly wrote: 'I left her a full fair lady, in mine eye at least the fairest, and when I returned I found her as foul a lady as the smallpox could make her, which she did take by the continual attendance of Her Majesty's most precious person, sick of the same disease.'

Lady Mary withdrew from the court, no doubt understanding that a badly disfigured lady of the bedchamber was not required. The queen certainly does not seem to have encouraged her to return. In

1578 Lady Mary paid a visit to Hampton Court, and found that she and her husband had only been allotted one room, which also had to serve as Sir Henry's office. Given the lack of accommodation at court this was perhaps not unusual, but since by this time Lady Mary was in bad health and spent a great deal of time in bed it hardly showed a great deal of royal gratitude for her sacrifice. Certainly her attempts to get better accommodation came to nothing.[30]

Rates of Pay and Conditions of Service

We no longer have complete records showing what court servants were paid throughout the Tudor period, and the evidence that does survive suggests that lady servants to royalty in particular were not paid a great deal in actual money. Elizabeth I's ladies of the privy chamber, the most socially elevated of her attendants, were not paid any salary at all, although of course they were only in occasional attendance. In Henry VIII's time the salaries of the maids of honour rose from £5 to £10.[31] Anne Basset was paid £10 a year when appointed as Jane Seymour's maid of honour in 1537.[32] By Elizabeth's reign the maids of honour were paid £40 a year, while at the beginning of the reign one of the ladies of the privy chamber was paid £34.[33] This was nothing like enough to make the post desirable just for the salary. It was impossible for a lady to play the star to her mistress's sun without a suitable wardrobe, and the cost of dressing for court was rising all the time in the sixteenth century, partly because of inflation and partly because of the increasing complexity of fashion at court.

The question of who exactly paid for the clothing for court ladies is a vexed one. The Lisle letters clearly show Anne Basset's family picking up the bill for most of her clothes. She had first become a maid of honour in Jane Seymour's time but went on to serve Henry's later queens as well. When she was first appointed maid of honour in 1537 she was told that she must have at least two gowns, one of satin and the other of (silk) damask.[34] But clothes of court standard did not come cheap. In 1557 a silk damask gown was made for

Thomasine Petre, daughter of William Petre (a royal secretary since the time of Henry VIII), which cost £8 for the damask silk alone and another 13*s* 4*d* to have it made up by the tailor. As far as we know, Thomasine never came to court and this fine gown was most likely her wedding dress.[35] Royal attendants, however, were frequently expected to dress in such style regularly which meant that their salaries didn't go far. If Anne Basset was typical, some of the expense of dressing for court was paid for by the king. Anne was given materials from the great wardrobe for Christmas and Whitsun, but this is unlikely to have been enough to cover her clothing for the whole year.[36] We know that the ladies were clothed at royal expense for ceremonial occasions such as royal funerals and coronations, when they drew black or scarlet cloth from the royal wardrobe. The men fared better, as they were mostly given official uniforms (liveries) which were definitely paid for by the king.[37]

We have some idea of the work involved in preparing and maintaining a daughter's wardrobe for her job as maid of honour from the letters which survive concerning Anne. There were standards to be met, as courtiers who held official posts were expected to be apparelled 'according to their degree', that is, according to the office they held. Anne, who had been brought up in France, was graciously allowed by the queen to wear out her French wardrobe before replacing it with English clothes. However, the flattering French hood was quite another matter; this had to be replaced with a velvet bonnet, which was described as 'becoming her nothing so well as the French hood'. Jane Seymour, who had been Anne Boleyn's maid of honour, had stolen Henry VIII from under her mistress's nose, and she did not want any of her maids of honour to repeat the process. In the end Anne's wardrobe included some of her mother's old clothes. In an age when cloth was precious even royalty recycled old clothes and Anne would have been in no place to complain.[38] In any case her chance for new clothes came soon enough. Anne came into royal service just before the birth of Prince Edward and a gown of black velvet edged with yellow satin had to be made for her at very short notice for the royal christening.[39]

The gentlemen, as might be expected in the sixteenth century, were paid rather more than the ladies. In 1519 the gentlemen of the privy chamber were given life annuities of £50 marks (a mark was 13*s* 4*d*).[40] In the Eltham Ordinances of 1525 they were paid £50 a year, and the grooms of the privy chamber £20 a year.

The actual pay was only part of the deal. One big advantage of working in the royal apartments was that you were given accommodation at court and ate at the royal expense. You were also given a number of other payments in kind, such as candles and wood for heating your lodgings. In times when both heating and lighting were expensive this was of some importance.

The accommodation was the most significant of these advantages. Accommodation at court was always at a premium and having a right to lodgings of some kind was privilege to be treasured. Of course, the lodgings available varied considerably. As we have seen, the domestic staff generally slept where they worked, and this was also true for the privy chamber staff. It was only when they were off duty that they had the luxury of sleeping in their private lodgings.

The private lodgings themselves varied a great deal. The most important royal servants could boast truly splendid lodgings. Thomas Cromwell seems to have had the use of St James's Palace when the court was at Whitehall, while Cavendish states that Wolsey was given the use of Richmond Palace, since the king was so impressed by the royal lodgings that Wolsey had built at Hampton Court. At Hampton Court itself there was also good provision for leading courtiers, with twenty-seven double lodgings, consisting of two rooms and a private privy. Again these were awarded to the fortunate few, such as Sir Anthony Browne (Master of the Horse), Princess Mary and Thomas Cromwell.[41]

Lesser accommodation consisted of a single room, or of shared rooms. Many found themselves living in far from luxurious circumstances. At Windsor the maids of honour, who seem to have generally shared a room, had to plead 'to have their chamber ceiled, and the partition that is of boards there to be made higher, for that the servants look over'.[42] The maids were also allowed accommodation for one servant each, so presumably they also had to be squeezed in somewhere.[43] So many people living in a relatively small space inevitably led to petty disputes, such as the problem of noisy neighbours. Nicholas L'Estrange, 1st Baron Hunstanton, recorded the following odd story:

> The Lord Knolls, in Queen Elizabeth's time, had his lodgings at Court, where some of the Ladyes and Maydes of Honour us'd to friske and hey about in the next roome, to his extreame disquiete a nights, though he had often warned them of it; at last he gets one to bold their owne backe doore, when they were all in one night at their revels, stripps off [to] his shirt, and with a payre of spectacles on his nose and Aretine in his hand, comes marching in at a posteren doore of his own chamber, reading very gravely, full upon the faces of them. Now let the reader judge what a sadd spectacle and pittifull fright these poore creatures endur'd, for the fac't them and often travesrst the roome in this posture above an houre.[44]

No doubt a certain amount of dramatic licence is used in this tale, but it does give an idea of the stresses of living in a very crowded court.

Court lodgings could also be used as another weapon in the constant war which the courtiers fought with one another. The duty of providing lodgings at court went through different hands in the sixteenth century, but in Elizabeth's time it was the Lord Chamberlain's responsibility. When Thomas Radcliffe, Earl of Sussex, held the post he delayed the return to court of Lady Mary Sidney by offering her only unsuitable lodgings. She, of course, was Robert Dudley's sister, and Sussex was trying to keep her away from the queen's privy chamber where she could have given crucial support to her brother. It was only when she protested to the queen that matters changed.[45] In the same way Cardinal Wolsey must have realised that his influence with the king was at an end when no lodgings could be found for him when the court was at Grafton, forcing him to ride 4 miles to another house late at night.[46] Grafton was one of the smaller royal houses, but men like Wolsey did not expect to be sent away. His worries were not unfounded, for his interview with the king at Grafton was to be the last.

The accommodation problem was complicated by the fact that the court moved from palace to palace. The largest palaces, like Whitehall and Hampton Court, posed no problem, but the smaller ones were a greater challenge. Of course, sometimes the smaller palaces were used by royalty precisely because they allowed them some peace and quiet – or at least the nearest thing to peace and quiet that they ever got. The king would visit them with his 'riding household', that is, the most necessary servants and his closest friends. The domestic servants who were not needed would be sent home on board wages until the court returned to somewhere larger, and those courtiers who weren't offered accommodation would go elsewhere. Indeed, not all those who were entitled to lodgings were allocated them at all the palaces. Thomas Howard, Duke of Norfolk, had rooms allocated for his use at nine different palaces, while others, such as the poet John Skelton, had rooms allocated to his permanent use only at Windsor.[47] At the smaller palaces even men such as Wolsey had no permanently allocated lodgings, hence the political wranglings over his accommodation at Grafton.

Another problem was that having large numbers of servants in attendance was an important status symbol at this time. It was simply impossible to provide lodgings at court for such large numbers of people, and Cardinal Wolsey had strictly regulated the numbers of servants that any member of the court was allowed to have lodged in a palace. This was obviously a serious problem, as the Eltham Ordinances are very firm about this matter: 'It is also the King's commandment, that the head officers of the household, the King and Queen's chambers, shall substantially foresee, that noe manner of persons, officers, or others, have or entertaine a greater number of servants in the court than be appointed or assigned unto them.'[48] Many courtiers had private houses close to the more important palaces so that they could lodge their extra servants outside the court and also enjoy the comforts of home if the overcrowding at court proved too much.

The greatest challenges on resources came when a royal visitor was expected, or when the court went on progress. The greatest royal visit of the sixteenth century was that paid by the Emperor Charles V in 1522. Such a man came complete with a huge entourage of attendants, all of whom had to be lodged in places befitting their station. The Rutland papers include a document concerning the visit, which contains all kinds of small details which had to be considered. There is a long list of suitable accommodation in London, belonging to everyone from courtiers to wealthy merchants, which was being commandeered, along with a note of the number of beds each could provide. There is a list of inns which had been inspected, with a view to stabling the huge number of horses that were expected. Beds were taken from various royal palaces, such as the Tower of London and Richmond, to furnish rooms for the emperor's train at Dover and Canterbury, where he would stop overnight on his way to London. Everything from pewter vessels and table linen to wax had to be obtained for the visitors. Under such circumstances members of the English court had to organise their own accommodation as best they could.[49]

A royal progress was a different matter. The Tudor monarch who enjoyed progress the most was definitely Elizabeth I, who seems to have regarded it as a summer holiday. The rest of the court felt differently.

The royal progress is often dismissed as a way by which Elizabeth could pass on to her subjects the cost of feeding the court. In fact, this was far from true. Cecil estimated that it cost somewhere in the region of £2,000 to transport the court, and in most cases the hosts did not pay. The slow rate of travel meant that frequently the queen was forced to stay in manor houses rather than great mansions and the owners of such houses simply could never have afforded to feed the entire court, even for a single night, so all such people were expected to provide was a clean and empty house. Towns and villages did have to provide food, fodder and fuel but these were paid for, even if at less than market prices. The main importance of the progress was as a public relations exercise. Even today, with all the huge amount of media exposure given to politicians, royalty and Hollywood stars, they all still recognise that a personal appearance boosts your popularity in a way that nothing else can. If the queen had ruined everyone she stayed with, the whole point of the exercise would have been lost. It was only the very rich and well connected who were expected to entertain the queen at their own expense – and it could indeed prove ruinous.

The progresses were very good at increasing the queen's popularity, but they were exceedingly hard work, both for those who had to organise them and for the rest of the court. The queen's ladies, however high in the royal favour they might be, had to sleep wherever there was room. When the queen was due to stay at the Archbishop of Canterbury's palace at Croydon in 1574 an officer wrote: 'I cannot tell where to place Mr Hatton, and for my Lady Carewe there is no place with a chimney for her but that must lie abroad by Mrs Parry and the rest of the Privy chamber. For Mrs Shelton here is no rooms with chimneys, I shall stay one chamber without for her. Here is as much as I have ways able to do in this house.'[50] The good news for the queen's ladies was that at least they were allocated rooms. Most of the court were left to organise their own accommodation on progress.

If court accommodation was the good side of royal service, the downside was the attendance that you were expected to give. In 1532 it was decreed that no more than five lodgings would be available for gentlemen of the privy chamber and that they should work on a rota of six weeks on duty followed by six weeks off. The intention was to keep down the numbers of people working in the privy chamber, and this would have been a sensible arrangement given that the king's attendants were all important men in their own right who had their own affairs to consider. However, as is so often the case, the theory and the practice were not quite the same. The gentlemen did not follow the rota, but came and went in a fairly random way. The problem was not necessarily the disobedience of the gentlemen, but rather the king's orders. He would send them off on various missions away from the court, and then complain that there was no one to wait on him. Under the circumstances there was no easy way to sort the situation out.[51]

Ladies working for queens seem to have had the opposite problem. Far from being sent away, their mistresses frequently simply refused to do without them. In 1575 Lady Cobham was evidently feeling the strain of the royal favour, as the Earl of Leicester reported that she wished to visit her husband at their country home 'to rest her weary bones awhile' but he obviously did not expect her request to be granted. This could be particularly wearing when Elizabeth was under pressure of some kind, when she would take out her problems on her ladies. In 1575, when she was worried by the war in the Netherlands, she even beat one or two of her ladies. Usually the violence was restricted to her tongue, which was so sarcastic and withering on such occasions that it could reduce her ladies to tears.[52]

The problem was particularly acute when the vexed matter of marriage arose. Elizabeth is famous for her dislike of seeing her ladies marry, but her sister Mary could be equally demanding. One of her favourite ladies was Jane Dormer, whom Mary would rarely allow to be absent from her side. Jane was offered a number of eligible husbands but of course could not marry without Mary's permission. Mary's answer, it seems, was usually that 'Jane Dormer deserved a very good husband' but that 'she knew not the man that was worthy of her'. The sixteenth-century manuscript from which this comes and the nineteenth-century book which was based on it are both keen to present Jane as some Tudor ideal of pious womanhood, and suggest that she didn't mind. You can't help but wonder if things were rather different in real life. In any case Jane did eventually marry the Spanish Duke of Feria, but not until Mary died.[53]

Most maids of honour, and indeed their families, were not prepared to forgo the prospect of marriage as easily as Jane Dormer is said to have done. It took a great deal of trouble and expense to place a girl as a maid of honour, as the problems around Anne Basset's wardrobe demonstrate. Families did not go to the trouble for nothing. Of course, such girls were expected to be the eyes and ears of their families in the royal apartments, and to use any opportunities that came their way to ask for favours of one kind and another for their families, but the idea was also that a girl displayed before the court in this way could expect to marry well.

Elizabeth's aversion to her ladies' marriages has perhaps been exaggerated. After all, during her reign thirteen of her maids of honour married peers, and she always stoutly maintained that it was only unsuitable marriages she objected to.[54] At some level Elizabeth's strict control of marriages was, after all, quite normal. Royalty had always been very careful to control aristocratic alliances, ensuring that no family could form bonds powerful enough to rival the crown. In the case of ladies such as Catherine Grey, who ended up in the Tower after marrying without royal permission, this was partly the case. Catherine had royal blood and so was a possible rival for the throne. Her case is certainly a sad one, but it is understandable given the ruthless nature of Renaissance politics.

The matches which infuriated Elizabeth the most were rash love-matches, which most Tudor parents discouraged anyway. There was an increasing feeling in the sixteenth century that marriages should be arranged between people who were reasonably compatible, but that matches based on love alone were a mistake. 'Hot love soon cools', the proverb ran.[55] These love-matches often took place between people who were not seen as social equals in sixteenth-century terms, and were regarded as a threat to the natural order. The queen was so infuriated when the Earl of Essex's sister Lady Dorothy Devereux ran away with the comparatively lowly Thomas Perrot and married him in a secret ceremony that even four years later she flew into a rage when she learnt that Dorothy was to be among the guests who would welcome her when she visited the Countess of Warwick at North Hall.[56] However, her attitude was not consistent, as sometimes she objected to marriages which were perfectly acceptable, such as that arranged between her cousin Catherine Carey and Lord Howard of Effingham's son Charles. Both sets of parents were entirely happy with the marriage and it was definitely a union of social equals, but the queen was so angry when she heard of it that both parties were dismissed from court. It went ahead anyway, and in this case Elizabeth did eventually come around to the idea, and took Catherine back into her service.[57]

Whatever Elizabeth's reasons, her attitude caused a great deal of scheming and secrecy among the maids of honour, who mostly married anyway, with or without royal permission. Fortunes among ladies who took their chances and married without royal permission varied. Elizabeth Throckmorton, who secretly married Walter Raleigh, was never accepted back at court despite having served the queen for seven years. Her husband, on the other hand, was allowed to resume his court career after a suitable period of disgrace. In 1594 the Countess of Rutland married off her daughter Lady Bridget Manners secretly, as Bridget was so much a favourite with the queen that the countess knew that permission for her to marry would never be granted. Bridget and her new husband Mr Tyrwhit were imprisoned, but only for a few months.

Some maids of honour had no one to blame but themselves when they were dismissed. There was a great deal of sexual temptation at court, given that there were so few unmarried ladies and so many well-bred, well-heeled men. In the circumstances it was inevitable that one or two of the less cautious maids of honour fell pregnant. Mary Fitton, who got pregnant by William Herbert, heir to the Earl of Pembroke, is an example. She was probably hoping for marriage, but Herbert not only had no intention of this but even rubbed salt into the wound by writing a moralistic verse for Mary, emphasising her folly. In an age when many felt that kings, not queens, should rule, Elizabeth had to be mindful of her reputation and could not dismiss such behaviour as youthful folly, even had she been sympathetic, which she definitely was not. Mary was sent away from the court, never to return.[58] Herbert was imprisoned for a while, but was allowed back to the court.

Even those who asked for permission to make a perfectly good marriage sometimes suffered for it. Mary Shelton, approaching the queen for permission to marry James Scudamore in 1576, found that her mistress 'dealt liberal both with blows and evil words', to the extent that she broke Mary's finger. Elizabeth herself realised that she had gone too far, so that she later not only agreed to the marriage but even promoted the new Lady Scudamore to a position in the privy chamber.[59]

The Benefits of Royal Personal Service

The benefits of royal service could be impressive indeed. Male servants attending a king obviously had the chance of being offered all kinds of lucrative jobs at both a local and national level, but ladies attending queens could benefit as well. At one level there was always a chance that the queen might bestow some fine presents on her attendants. Jane Seymour, for example, gave jewelled girdles to her ladies of the privy chamber.[60] Gifts of clothing were not unusual, especially when the ladies were all expected to dress in the same way for some occasion. In 1565 six maids of honour were given yellow satin gowns by the queen to wear at the wedding of Lady Anne Russell, daughter of the Earl of Bedford, to the Earl of Warwick.[61] At the same time Lady Anne herself was presented with a very fine gown, one which the queen herself had once worn and which was now remade for her. It was made of cloth of tissue (which would have been made with either gold or silver thread) and purple velvet, embroidered with gold and lined with gold taffeta. In fact, Elizabeth was very generous with gifts of clothing and often made them to her ladies-in-waiting in particular.[62] The queen also gave away old gowns from her wardrobe to her ladies, but exactly how they were allocated nobody knows. Given the cost of valuable fabrics at this time, these gifts were more generous than we might consider today.[63]

This gift-giving was not all one way, as at New Year Elizabeth I's ladies were often expected to present their mistress with gifts. The 'official' gift expected on this occasion was a purse with a certain amount of gold in it, in return for which the giver would be given goods worth a certain amount according to their position, usually in the form of plate. Those closest to the queen soon found that she preferred more personal gifts and often presented valuable jewels, sometimes with the hidden meanings which the Elizabethans loved so much. In 1587 Sir Francis Drake gave Elizabeth a fan with a gold handle on which was a half-moon set with mother of pearl, with a smaller one inside it set with diamonds. On the other side was the queen's picture and seed pearls. The half-moon was the symbol of Diana, the chaste moon goddess, to whom Elizabeth was frequently compared in both art and literature.[64] Garments were also very acceptable and Elizabeth was frequently given either complete gowns or items such as sets of sleeves and petticoats. Again an apt choice was particularly admired. In 1587 the Lord Admiral gave her a 'Sea Capp of black velvet, Imbrothered all over with shippes and Ankers of ragged pearle of sondrie sortes'.[65] Whatever the cost, if they resulted in the giver gaining considerable influence with the queen, it was well worth paying.

Using your influence with the queen to secure jobs, pardons and other favours for relatives, friends and those prepared to pay for your services could be lucrative indeed. Although Elizabeth absolutely forbade her ladies to become involved in politics, she accepted that granting these sorts of favours via her ladies was all part of how the court worked. Her ladies were not slow to take advantage and could drive a hard bargain. Dorothy, Lady Edmunds, was certainly able to demonstrate this to Anthony Bacon in 1595. The case is also a very good example of the court at work, and shows why getting anything done cost so much money.

Bacon had been offered £100 and a bond of £500, which would pay out £300 immediately, if he would secure a pardon from the queen for a certain Robert Boothe. Whether Mr Boothe deserved his pardon or not we do not know, and it was in this case beside the point, as he could afford to pay. Bacon's agent at court, Anthony Standen, was given the task of trying to find someone who would approach the queen on the matter, with the original £100 as a reward. Lady Edmunds agreed to do so, provided that the Lord Chamberlain, who did not like Boothe, agreed. On approaching the Lord Chamberlain she found him ready to agree, but claimed that he had advised her that she would be unwise to make her suit for less than £1,000. Standen explained to Bacon in a letter that Lady Edmunds said that 'the manner of the queen is to ask what the suit will be worth, so that naming the £100, which is the sum I offered her, she says the queen will not be moved with it for so small a matter to employ her credit and forces she will not'.

Bacon was then trapped. Lady Edmunds was expecting too much, but he could not go to another member of the privy chamber who might work for less money, because Lady Edmunds would use her influence to see that the pardon was not granted.[66]

This incident hardly shows the court in a favourable light but it does demonstrate that Elizabeth's ladies could turn their position to their advantage with just as much skill as any male courtier. If the men of the court often complained that the ladies' offers of help frequently came to nothing (see the comments of Robert Cross above for an example), it must be remembered that all courtiers' offers of help often came to nothing, whatever their sex.

Personal service to the monarch was certainly a prize to hang on to, as certain families served several generations of the royal family and did all they could to find places for other relatives. By Elizabeth's time the royal privy chamber was almost a closed shop with families such as the Howards, Careys, Radcliffes and Knollys taking most of the positions. A couple of hardy people also served Elizabeth throughout her long reign. They were Dorothy Edmunds, a gentlewoman of the privy chamber and one of the grooms, Henry Sackford.[67]

Fortunately, due to the survival of the Lisle letters, we have some idea of what was involved in preparing your daughter for royal service and what negotiations were necessary to try to win for her an elusive post in the royal privy chamber. It does not seem that all the girls of the family were intended for the court. Confidence, good looks and a clever wit were necessary if a girl was to flourish at court. Anne's mother, Lady Lisle, may well have considered the court as a possibility for Anne quite early on as, aged about twelve or thirteen, she was sent into the household of a French noblewoman. As we have already observed, language skills were important at court and the French were also considered to have elegant social manners. Anne remained in this household for almost three years. The politics of trying to get her a position at court seem to have taken around a year, starting in 1536 and ending when Anne was appointed in September 1537.

An enormous amount of work achieved Anne her post. One thing that becomes immediately obvious from reading the letters is the importance of the influence of two ladies, Lady Sussex (Anne's cousin) and Lady Rutland, who was Lord Lisle's cousin once removed. Connections at court were always vital to achieving jobs there and what seem quite distant connections to us were often pressed into service. In the end it was a gift of quail that finally led to Anne's appointment. Gifts changed hands frequently in Tudor times, and were definitely not limited to 'official' gift-giving periods such as New Year. They were part of the cement which held society together. As you might expect, gifts were sometimes lavish but smaller, homely items also changed hands. The Lisle letters see Lady Lisle sending conserves to Lady Sussex, which are much appreciated.[68] Even royalty happily received such items. The gift which finally led to Anne Basset's appointment was not some lavish jewel but a simple gift of plump quail. Jane Seymour, who was pregnant at the time, had developed a craving for quail, which fortunately Lady Lisle was able to provide. Lady Sussex and Lady Rutland were waiting on the queen when she was eating them, and used the opportunity to drop Anne's name at the right moment. Even then Anne was not given the job immediately, but had to come to court for the queen to see her in person before she was finally 'sworn the Queen's maid'.[69]

The Daily Routine

The daily routine of working in the royal apartments obviously varied depending on who the monarch was, and their age. For example, as a young man Henry VIII was constantly out hunting or taking part in some sport, but as he aged he found such activity much less appealing and spent more time in his private apartments. In the same way the ladies who attended his queens had to adapt to their varying tastes. Several ladies served all six queens and had to master everything from the strict religious devotion of Catherine of Aragon to the livelier tastes of Katherine Howard. This was no small matter. Here is an account of Catherine of Aragon's religious devotions:

> She rose at mid-night to be present at the matins of the Religious. At five o'clock she made herself ready with what haste she might, saying that the time was lost which was spent in apparelling herself. . . . She fasted all Fridays and Saturdays and all the Eves of our Blessed Lady with bread and water. On Sundays she received the Blessed Sacrament, read the daily Office of the Blessed Virgins, she was the most part of the morning in the Church at holy service and after dinner read the life of that day's Saint to her maids standing by. Then she returned to the Church. . . .[70]

Her ladies were of course expected to follow their mistress in all this, which must have been distinctly tedious for those who were less religiously inclined.

Despite the inevitable variations, a good idea of the daily round in the royal apartments can be obtained from the Eltham Ordinances. The routine was not particularly taxing by the standards of the time. The pages of the chamber (that is, the great chamber) had to be up and about by seven 'or soone after',[71] which was luxury considering that most other workers were expected to be up and ready at five or six. They then had to make up the fires and rouse the squires of the body so that they could be ready in the king's chamber by eight at the latest. The esquires had their own servants to attend them, of course, but they were not allowed to go into the pallet chamber where their masters slept when on duty. Instead the pages had to carry the esquires' clothes between them and their servants. This was to discourage any unauthorised people from entering the royal private apartments.[72]

This, at least, was the theory. The esquires were men of some importance, and were evidently aware of the fact. The pages clearly had problems getting them out of bed because the ordinances go on to state that if they are not up and ready in time 'then immediately when they are up, they shall depart out of the king's chamber in their night gownes to such chamber as is assigned unto them in the court by the gentlemen ushers'. In other words, they had to get out of the way and dress elsewhere so as not to hinder the preparation of the king and his apartments for the day ahead. Evidently they were not all prepared to oblige, as the ordinances go on to say that the pages should report any who refused to do so to the Lord Chamberlain, who would consider a punishment. You can't help wondering how many pages were either brave or foolish enough to risk offending such an important person by reporting him to the Lord Chamberlain.[73]

The yeoman ushers, who kept the door of the king's great (or outer) chamber, were to be on duty by eight. They had strict instructions not to leave their post unless another yeoman usher took over from them, and their job was to keep out everyone but 'lords, knights, gentlemen officers of the King's house and other honest personages'.[74] Of course, 'honest personages' was a term open to some interpretation, so they were supposed to refer all doubtful cases to the Lord Chamberlain or the Vice-Chamberlain. They must have displayed a great deal of tact to avoid offending delicate courtier egos. A good yeoman usher must certainly have been prepared to make himself unpopular, because they also had the job of enforcing good behaviour in the great chamber and of seeing that no gambling took place there. The Tudors loved gambling and the long hours spent waiting around at court had to be filled somehow.

The grooms of the privy chamber were the first people to get up in the king's private rooms. They were not considered grand enough to sleep in the privy chamber, but were to be up, ready and in the apartments to start work between six and seven 'or sooner'.[75] Their hours really depended on the king's wishes. As they were basically the cleaning staff the idea was that their work was done by the time the king was up, even if he was up early. They had to clear away the pallets that the gentlemen of the privy chamber slept on, make up the fires and generally make the chamber 'pure, cleane, whollsome and meete'.

We might imagine that the relatively lowly grooms would have been awed into doing their work quickly, efficiently and willingly, but again the court regulations suggest that the reality was rather different. The grooms are reminded that they should perform their work 'without grudge, contradiction or disdaine', intimating that they felt such manual work was rather beneath them. In fact, they had even been sending their own servants to clean the privy chamber, which was very much against the royal intentions. One of the reasons the Eltham Ordinances were drawn up in the first place was that the royal private apartments were becoming increasingly less private, so the last thing the king wanted was the servants of his own servants wandering around in his private rooms. The grooms' servants were henceforth banned from the privy chamber and the grooms reminded that they had better perform their own work themselves.[76]

The two gentlemen of the privy chamber who were on duty had to be up by seven at the latest, or sooner if the king had told them that he wanted to be up earlier. Only the gentlemen were allowed 'to lay hands up his royall person' so obviously they had to be up, ready and dressed by the time the king wished to rise. The yeomen of the wardrobe would bring the king's clothes as far as the privy chamber door, but they were not allowed to enter. Instead, they passed the royal clothes to the gentlemen. In the same way, if the king wanted a snack between meals, food and drink was brought to the privy chamber and then handed over to the gentlemen to give to the king.[77]

A great deal of time at court was taken up by meals. If the king was at one of his larger palaces, where 'hall was kept' (i.e. dining was done in public with everyone sitting in their allotted place), then the first of the two sittings for dinner for the household was at ten or even 'somewhat afore' and the first sitting of supper at four on weekdays, or 'after the King be gone to the chapel' for both dinner and supper on Sundays. Where hall was not kept, in smaller palaces, dinner was at eleven and supper at six, although the regulations point out that the king and queen were always at liberty to dine exactly when it suited them.[78]

If the king was having either dinner or supper in his own dining chamber, as he usually did, the Lord Chamberlain (or Vice-Chamberlain in his absence) had to be present until the king was actually ready to start eating. At that point the Lord Chamberlain and all the other courtiers who did not have an official part to play in serving the king left the room and had their own dinner. The Lord Chamberlain and those who dined at his table would sit down and then the ushers would clear the room of all those who were not to either dine or serve. It was all a complicated business.[79]

In theory, everyone was seated at a table and in a place fitting for his rank as part of the endless status game that the Tudors loved to play, and which the court particularly excelled in. It was also a way of making the court look its most impressive, with all the grandest courtiers dining in public (or semi-public) places. This system also made it easier to see that everyone got the food that they were officially allowed, which was, after all, part of their pay. However, as was so often the case, the glittering image of the court and the rather more disorganised reality were rather different. The Ordinances state that 'sundry noblemen, gentlemen and others doe much delight and use to dyne in corners and secret places, not repaireing to the King's chamber nor hall' and, as noted before, the problem was never really resolved during the Tudor period.[80] The only people to whom the rules did not apply were privy chamber staff. As we have seen, both the king and queen had private kitchens, partly so that they could eat when it suited them. The privy chamber staff were expected to wait upon the king at meals, so special provision was made for them so that they could fit their dining around the king.

Another focal part of the day was attending church services. As noted before, this was considered an important part of life among the nobility. Among royalty it was even more necessary. When the monarch was keeping full court at one of the larger palaces, going to chapel would be done in great state and was known as the 'Coming Forth'. The idea was that the monarch had a chance to show themselves off to the court on their way to the chapel. It was quite necessary that they did this. First of all, they needed to show to the world that they were alive and well and still very much in control. Now that the monarch had retreated into more genuinely private apartments than had existed in previous centuries, the bulk of the court, who were not admitted to this exclusive realm, needed to know this important fact. Royal deaths could be hushed up, at least for a short time. When Henry VIII died his death was kept quiet for three days. This was a result partly of the debate over the fate of the Duke of Norfolk, who was due to be executed on the morning that Henry actually died, and partly of the complex political scheming over the setting up of a regency for the young Edward VI.[81]

The other important reason for the Coming Forth was that it allowed courtiers access to the monarch. If they could attract the royal eye, they could present their petition directly to them, without having to go to the time and expense of getting a courtier to obtain an audience for them. It was in the monarch's interests to remind people that they, and not even the most important courtiers, were the true source of power and patronage.

Since it was mostly a public relations exercise, the Coming Forth was done in style. Here is a description of Elizabeth I coming forth, as described by Paul Hentzner, who was obviously as impressed by this ceremony as he was by the serving of the queen's dinner. The setting was the presence chamber at Greenwich, and the queen came out of her private apartments in great state:

> First went Gentlemen, Barons, Earls, Knights of the Garter, all richly dressed and bare-headed; next came the Chancellor, bearing

the Seals in a red-silk Purse, between Two Gentlemen; one of which carried the Royal Scepter, the other the Sword of State, in a red scabbard, studded with golden Fleurs de Lis, the point upwards; Next came the Queen, in the Sixty-fifth Year of her Age, as we were told, very majestic; her Face oblong, fair, but wrinkled; her Eyes small, yet black and pleasant; her Nose a little hooked; her Lips narrow, and her Teeth black; (a defect the English seem subject to, from their too great use of sugar); she had in her Ears two pearls, with very rich drops; she wore false Hair, and that red; upon her Head she had a small Crown, reported to be made of some of the gold of the celebrated Lunebourg table: Her Boson was uncovered, as all the English ladies have it, till they marry; and she had on a Necklace of exceeding fine jewels; her Hands were small, her Fingers long, and her Stature neither tall nor low; her air was stately, her manner of speaking mild and obliging. That day she was dressed in white Silk, bordered with pearls the size of beans, and over it a Mantle of black silk, shot with silver threads; her Train was very long, the end of it borne by a Marchioness; instead of a Chain, she had an oblong Collar of gold and jewels. As she went along in all this state and magnificence, she spoke very graciously, first to one, then to another, whether foreign Ministers, or those who attended for different reasons, in English, French and Italian; for besides being well skilled in Greek, Latin and the Languages I have mentioned, she is mistress of Spanish, Scotch, and Dutch: Whoever speaks to her, it is kneeling; now and then she raises some with her Hand. While we were there, W. Slawata, a Bohemian Baron, had letters to present to her; and she, after pulling off her glove, gave him her right Hand to kiss, sparkling with rings and jewels, a mark of particular Favour: Wherever she turned her Face, as she was going along, every body fell down on their knees. The Ladies of the Court followed next to her, very handsome and well shaped, and for the most part dressed in white; she was guarded on each side by the Gentlemen Pensioners, fifty in number, with guild battle-axes; in the Antichapel next the Hall where we were, Petitions

> were presented to her, and she received them most graciously, which occasioned the acclamation of 'Long live Queen Elizabeth!' She answered it with 'I thank you my good people'.[82]

It is evident from the description that Hentzner was deeply impressed by all of this, proving the worth of such theatre in the court.

After such an elaborate ceremony, you can imagine Elizabeth being only too glad to retire to the privacy of her private apartments when it was over. Supper was less formal than dinner and was a meal that the monarch might choose to share with friends in private. The final ceremony of the day, as in any great household, was the 'All Night'. If the rules set up by Henry VII were still in force, this started with the elaborate making of the royal bed, which was even sprinkled with holy water as part of the process.[83] After this, as soon as they had put their royal master or mistress to bed, the privy chamber staff who were on duty could then go to bed in the pallet chamber, while the others left for their own lodgings. Another day at court was over.

Notes

INTRODUCTION

1. Lawrence Stone, *The Crisis of the Aristocracy, 1558–1641* (Oxford University Press, 1967), p. 101.
2. *Ibid.*, p. 102.
3. *Ibid.*, p. 103.
4. Anne Somerset, *Elizabeth I* (Phoenix Paperbacks, 1991), p. 345.
5. C.M. Barron, 'Centres of Conspicuous Consumption: The Aristocratic Town House in London 1200–1550', *London Journal* 20 (1995).
6. Stone, *Crisis of the Aristocracy*, p. 251.

ONE: GOLDSMITHS, FULLERS AND DYERS

1. Mercers dealt in fine-quality fabrics, such as silks.
2. O. Jocelyn Dunlop, *English Apprenticeship and Child Labour* (T. Fisher Unwin, 1912), p. 70.
3. Walter Sherburne Prideaux (ed.), *Memorials of the Goldsmiths' Company 1335–1815* (Eyre & Spottiswoode, n.d.), p. 38.
4. *Ibid.*, pp. 38 and 53.
5. J.R. Boyle and F.W. Dendy (eds), *Extracts from the Records of the Merchant Adventurers of Newcastle-upon-Tyne* (Surtees Society, 1895), vol. 1, p. 24.
6. Dunlop, *English Apprenticeship and Child Labour*, p. 37.
7. *Ibid.*, p. 43.
8. *Ibid.*, p. 45.
9. Sherburne Prideaux, *Memorials of the Goldsmiths' Company*, p. 28.
10. Dunlop, *English Apprenticeship and Child Labour*, p. 45.
11. *Ibid.*, p. 51.
12. *Ibid.*, p. 57.
13. *Ibid.*, p. 58.

14. *Ibid.*, p. 46.
15. Anne Daly (ed.), *Kingston upon Thames Apprentices 1563–1713* (Surrey Record Society, 1994).
16. For more information see Sylvia L. Thrupp, *The Merchant Class of Medieval London* (University of Michigan Press, 1977), p. 164.
17. Boyle and Dendy (eds), *Merchant Adventurers of Newcastle-upon-Tyne*, vol. 1, p. 20.
18. For examples of some Renaissance etiquette books, see F.J. Furnivall (ed.), *The Babees Book* (Chatto & Windus, 1923).
19. Sherburne Prideaux, *Memorials of the Goldsmiths' Company*, p. 37.
20. Thrupp, *Merchant Class of Medieval London*, p. 166.
21. Dunlop, *English Apprenticeship and Child Labour*, p. 179.
22. For the full story, see Janet Arnold, *Queen Elizabeth's Wardrobe Unlock'd* (W.S. Maney & Son, 1988), p. 159.
23. Sherburne Prideaux, *Memorials of the Goldsmiths' Company*, p. 58.
24. *Ibid.*
25. *Ibid.*, p. 48.
26. Dunlop, *English Apprenticeship and Child Labour*, p. 36.
27. Sherburne Prideaux, *Memorials of the Goldsmiths' Company*, p. 94.
28. Dunlop, *English Apprenticeship and Child Labour*, p. 56.
29. Quoted from Barbara Winchester, *Tudor Family Portrait* (Jonathan Cape, 1955), p. 130. The original letters can now be found in The National Archives at Kew.
30. *Ibid.*, p. 224.
31. Dunlop, *English Apprenticeship and Child Labour*, p. 47.
32. Daly (ed.), *Kingston upon Thames Apprentices*, pp. 10, 11 and 8 respectively.
33 Dunlop, *English Apprenticeship and Child Labour*, pp. 150–1.
34. Sue Wright, 'Churmaids, Huswyfes and Hucksters. The Employment of Women in Tudor and Stuart Salisbury', in C. Linsey and L. Duffen (eds), *Women and Work in Pre-Industrial England* (Croom Helm, 1985).
35. Sherburne Prideaux, *Memorials of the Goldsmiths' Company*, p. 64.
36. Dunlop, *English Apprenticeship and Child Labour*, p. 146.
37. *Ibid.*, p. 60.

TWO: JOHN BLANK COMES TO COURT

1. F.O. Shyllon, *Black Slaves in Britain* (Oxford University Press for the Institute of Race Relations, 1974), p. 2.
2. *Calendar of State Papers Domestic*, 1597, 7 April, 104.

3. Peter Fryer, *Staying Power. The History of Black People in Britain* (Pluto Press, 1984), p. 8.
4. *Ibid.*, p. 9.
5. *Ibid.*, p. 10. See also James Walvin, *The Black Presence* (Orbach and Chambers, 1971), pp. 64–5.
6. Fryer, *Staying Power*, p. 5. See also Richard Hakluyt, *The Principall Navigations, Voiages, Traffiques and Discoveries of the English Nation* (London, 1598), vol. 2.
7. Eldred D. Jones, *The Elizabethan Image of Africa* (University Press of Virginia for Folger Shakespeare Library, 1971), p. 41.
8. For an admittedly rather poor reproduction of the painting see Sewter, 'Queen Elizabeth at Kenilworth', *Burlington Magazine* lxxvi, April 1940. The information regarding the setting of the picture and the identification in the article of some of the figures in the painting is questioned in later correspondence to the magazine, but the occasion is obviously a fashionable, aristocratic one.
9. Fryer, *Staying Power*, pp. 2–4.
10. *Ibid.*, p. 6.
11. Gretchen Gerzine, *Black London* (Rutgers University Press, 1995), p. 5.
12. For more information on travel literature published in the sixteenth century see Louis B. Wright, *Middle Class Culture in Elizabethan England* (Cornell University Press for Folger Shakespeare Library, 1935), and also Jones, *Elizabethan Image of Africa*.

THREE: HOUSEWIVES, HUSBANDMEN AND PLOUGHMEN

1. See Ann Kussmaul, *Servants in Husbandry in Early Modern England* (Cambridge University Press, 1981).
2. Joan Thirsk (ed.), *Chapters from the Agrarian History of England and Wales 1500–1750* (Cambridge University Press, 1990), vol. 2, *Rural Society – Landowners, Peasants and Labourers, 1500–1750,* p. 66.
3. Kussmaul, *Servants in Husbandry*, p. 39.
4. *Ibid.*, pp. 36–7.
5. Joan Thirsk (ed.), *The Rural Economy of England. Collected Essays* (Hambledon Press, 1984), p. 377.
6. Thirsk (ed.), *Chapters from the Agrarian History of England and Wales*, vol. 1, ed. Peter J. Bowden, *Economic Change – Prices, Wages, Profits and Rents 1500–1750,* p. 18.
7. For full details of regional variations see Thirsk (ed.) *Chapters from the Agrarian History of England and Wales*, vol. 5, *The Buildings of the Countryside.*

8. William Harrison, *The Description of England*, ed. Georges Edelen (Folger Shakespeare Library and Dover Publications, 1994), p. 197.
9. Thirsk (ed.), *Chapters from the Agrarian History of England and Wales*, vol. 5, *The Buildings of the Countryside*, p. 55.
10. *Ibid.*, p. 70.
11. Thomas Tusser's *A Hundreth Points of Husbandrie* was published in London in 1557. He later expanded it into *Five Hundreth Points of Good Husbandrie*, the work for which he is best known. Both are written in very bad but very memorable verse. The edition of *Hundred Points* quoted from here was printed by Da Capo Press in 1973, while the edition of *Five Hundred Points* was printed for the English Dialect Society by Truber & Co. in 1878.
12. Gervase Markham, *The English Housewife*, ed. Michael R. Best (McGill-Queens University Press, 1986), pp. 7–8.
13. Harrison, *Description of England*, p. 117.
14. Markham, *English Housewife*, p. 170.
15. For full details of Tudor cheese-making, see Markham, *English Housewife*.
16. For a more detailed description of sixteenth-century agriculture explained in modern terms, see Thirsk (ed.), *Chapters from the Agrarian History of England and Wales*, vol. 3, *Agricultural Change: Policy and Practice 1500–1750*.
17. Kussmaul, *Servants in Husbandry*, p. 32.
18. *Ibid.*
19. *Ibid.*, p. 48.
20. *Ibid.*, p. 41.
21. *Ibid.*, p. 33.
22. Thirsk (ed.), *Chapters from the Agrarian History of England and Wales*, vol. 2, *Rural Society*, p. 69.
23. Ralph Houlbrooke, *The English Family 1450–1700* (Longman, 1984), pp. 66–7.
24. Thirsk (ed.), *Chapters from the Agrarian History of England and Wales*, vol. 2, *Rural Society*, p. 163.
25. For more information on the economic situation at this time see Thirsk (ed.), *Chapters from the Agrarian History of England and Wales*, vol. 1, ed. Bowden, *Economic Change – Prices, Wages, Profits and Rents 1500–1750*.

FOUR: LORDS AND LADIES, BISHOPS AND PRINCES

1. Kate Mertes, *The English Noble Household* (Basil Blackwell, 1988), p. 64.
2. *Ibid.*, p. 57.
3. *Ibid.*, p. 43.

4. Muriel St Clare Byrne (ed.), *The Lisle Letters* (Penguin Books, 1985), p. 132.
5. C.M. Woolgar, *The Great Household in Late Medieval England* (Yale University Press, 1999), p. 85.
6. R.G.K.A. Mertes, 'The Household as a Religious Community', in J. Rosenthal and Colin Richmond (eds), *People, Politics and Community in the Later Middle Ages* (Alan Sutton, 1987), p. 125.
7. *Ibid.*
8. Felicity Heal, *Hospitality in Early Modern England* (Clarendon Press, 1990), p. 43.
9. Instructions for the full ceremony can be found in John Russell, *The Book of Courtesy*, in F.J. Furnivall (ed.), *The Babees Book* (Ballantyne Press, 1923), pp. 102–4.
10. Mertes, 'Household as a Religious Community', p. 134.
11. Mertes, *English Noble Household*, pp. 64 and 190.
12. Jennifer Woodward, *The Theatre of Death* (Boydell Press, 1997), p. 6. The full description of the Earl of Derby's funeral can be found here.
13. A bannerol is a narrow forked flag, attached to a staff or lance.
14. Richard C. Barnett, *Place, Profit and Power*, James Sprunt Studies in History and Political Science (University of North Carolina Press, 1969), p. 19.

FIVE: YEOMEN, SCULLIONS AND CHILDREN

1. John Russell, *The Book of Nurture*, in F.J. Furnivall (ed.), *Bokes of Nurture and Keruynge* (London, 1867), p. 79.
2. Mertes, *English Noble Household*, p. 17.
3. Russell, *Book of Courtesy*, pp. 120–1.
4. Mertes, *English Noble Household*, p. 67.
5. 'The Eltham Ordinances, cap. 37', in *Ordinances for the Royal Household from Edward III to William and Mary* (Society of Antiquaries of London, 1790), p. 147.
6. C.M. Woolgar, *The Great Household in Late Medieval England* (Yale University Press, 1999), p. 63.
7. Russell, *Book of Courtesy*, p. 92.
8. 'Ordinances for the Household of Princess Cecill', in *Ordinances for the Royal Household*, p. 39.
9. 'The Eltham Ordinances: A diet for the Wardrober of the beds, Groom Porter, yeoman and Officers of the House of like fare', in *Ordinances for the Royal Household*, p. 173.
10. 'The Eltham Ordinances: A Diet . . . to the maides, servants, children of the offices, porters and skowerers', in *Ordinances for the Royal Household*, p. 190.

11. Russell, *Book of Courtesy*, p. 82.
12. *The Ship of Fools*, trans. Alexander Barclay (William Paterson (Edinburgh) and Henry Sotheran (London), 1874), p. 264.
13. F.G. Emmison, *Tudor Secretary: Sir William Petre at Court and Home* (Longmans, 1961), p. 152.
14. 'The Eltham Ordinances, cap. 37', in *Ordinances for the Royal Household*, p. 148.
15. George Cavendish, *The Life and Death of Cardinal Wolsey*, ed. R.S. Sylvester (Oxford University Press, 1961), pp. 21–2.
16. F.J. Furnivall, *A Dyetary of Helth*, ed. Andrew Boorde (Early English Text Society, 1906), p. 236.
17. *Ibid.*, pp. 236 and 239.
18. Simon Thurley, *The Royal Palaces of Tudor England* (Yale University Press, 1993), p. 174.
19. For more information on sanitation in royal palaces, see *ibid.*, chapter 10.
20. Furnivall, *Dyetary of Helth*, pp. 236–7.
21. Thurley, *Royal Palaces*, p. 174.
22. Furnivall, *Dyetary of Helth*, pp. 51–3.
23. Woolgar, *Great Household*, p. 169.
24. Peter Brears, *All the King's Cooks* (Souvenir Press, 1999), p. 177.
25. Russell, *Book of Nurture*, p. 51.
26. Russell, *Book of Courtesy*, p. 81.
27. Mertes, *English Noble Household*, p. 39.
28. 'Ordinances for the Household of the Duke of Clarence', in *Ordinances for the Royal Household*, p. 89.
29. 'The Eltham Ordinances, cap. 38', in *Ordinances for the Royal Household*, p. 148.
30. Emmison, *Tudor Secretary*, p. 132.
31. Mertes, *English Noble Household*, p. 132.
32. Woolgar, *Great Household*, p. 113.
33. David Loades, *The Tudor Court* (Headstart History, 1992), p. 72.
34. Woolgar, *Great Household*, p. 114.
35. Brears, *All the King's Cooks*, p. 102.
36. *Ibid.*, p. 101.
37. Francis Bacon, *Essayes or Cunsels Civill and Moral* (J.M. Dent, 1899), p. 171.
38. Cavendish, *Life and Death of Cardinal Wolsey*, pp. 70–1.
39. Brears, *All the King's Cooks*, pp. 66–7.
40. Emmison, *Tudor Secretary*, p. 145.
41. Barbara Winchester, *Tudor Family Portrait* (Jonathan Cape, 1955), p. 142.

42. A haberdin was a kind of large cod, salted or sun-dried.
43. Thurley, *Royal Palaces*, p. 157.

SIX: HENCHMEN, HONOUR AND HOSPITALITY

1. For details of how to lay the table see Russell, *Book of Nurture*, pp. 52–4.
2. *Ibid.*, p. 76.
3. Kenneth Charlton, *Education in Renaissance England* (Routledge & Kegan Paul, 1965), p. 220.
4. *Ibid.*, 'The Renaissance Debate in England', for more detail.
5. 'Liber Niger Domus Regis Edward IV', p. 45, in *Ordinances for the Royal Household.*
6. Nicholas Orme, *From Childhood to Chivalry* (Methuen, 1984), p. 57.
7. William Nelson (ed.), *A Fifteenth-Century School Book* (Clarendon Press, 1956).
8. Roger Ascham, *The Schoolmaster* (Cassell & Co., 1909), p. 15.
9. Nelson, *Fifteenth-Century School Book*, p. 30.
10. See 'The Oxford Notebook', in Charlton, *Education in Renaissance England*, p. 130.
11. Orme, *From Childhood to Chivalry*, p. 118.
12. *Ibid.*, p. 128.
13. Joan Simon, *Education and Society in Tudor England* (Cambridge University Press, 1966), p. 347.
14. William Gryndall, *Hawking, Hunting, Fouling and Fishing with the True Measures of Blowing* (London, 1596) – one of the many books on sport based on *The Book of St Albans.*
15. Charlton, *Education in Renaissance England*, p. 220.
16. For more information on Christopher Hatton, see Eric St John Brooks, *Sir Christopher Hatton* (Jonathan Cape, 1946).
17. Cavendish, *Life and Death of Cardinal Wolsey*, p. xvii.
18. Simon, *Education and Society in Tudor England*, p. 356.
19. *Ibid.*, p. 354.
20. For more information, see Alison Sim, *The Tudor Housewife* (Sutton Publishing, 1996), p. 40.
21. *Ibid.*
22. Karen Robertson, 'Tracing a Woman's Connections from a Letter', in Susan Grye and Karen Robertson (eds), *Maids and Mistresses, Cousins and Queens* (Oxford University Press, 1999).
23. Orme, *From Childhood to Chivalry*, p. 60.
24. For information on the post of usher, see Russell, *Book of Courtesy*, p. 97 and *Book of Nurture*, pp. 73–5.

25. Woolgar, *Great Household*, p. 154.
26. For more information on the subject of hospitality, see Heal, *Hospitality in Early Modern England.*
27. For information on the business interests of the sixteenth-century aristocracy, see Stone, *Crisis of the Aristocracy.*
28. Lawrence Stone, *Family and Fortune* (Clarendon Press, 1973), p. 181.
29. Stone, *Crisis of the Aristocracy*, p. 293.
30. Stone, *Family and Fortune*, p. 169.
31. *Ibid.*, pp. 190–2.
32. Stone, *Crisis of the Aristocracy*, p. 351.
33. *Ibid.*, p. 377.
34. *Ibid.*, pp. 357–60.
35. Stone, *Family and Fortune*, pp. 11–12.
36. Stone, *Crisis of the Aristocracy*, p. 363.
37. *Ibid.*, p. 461.
38. *Ibid.*, p. 376.
39. *Ibid.*, section on 'Estate Management'.
40. Barnett, *Place, Profit and Power*, p. 16.
41. *Ibid.*, pp. 17–18.
42. Cavendish, *Life and Death of Cardinal Wolsey*, pp. xxiv–xxvi.
43. For more information on Michael Hickes, see Alan G.R. Smith, *Servant of the Cecils* (Jonathan Cape, 1977).
44. Henry Percy, Earl of Northumberland, *Advice to His Son*, quoted from Muriel St Clare Byrne (ed.), *The Lisle Letters* (University of Chicago Press, 1981), vol. 3, p. 23.
45. Cavendish, *Life and Death of Cardinal Wolsey*, p. xxi.

SEVEN: STARS IN THE PRESENCE OF THE SUN

1. Thurley, *Royal Palaces*. All the information on the physical appearance of the royal apartments comes from this book unless otherwise stated.
2. Nicholas Richard Turpyn, *The Chronicle of Calais*, ed. John Gough (Camden Society, 1846).
3. David Starkey, *The English Court* (Longman, 1987), pp. 75–6.
4. Loades, *Tudor Court*, p. 47.
5. Starkey, *English Court*, p. 46.
6. 'The Eltham Ordinances, cap. 55', in *Ordinances for the Royal Household*, p. 154.
7. Starkey, *English Court*, p. 86.
8. *Ibid.*, p. 87.

9. *Ibid.*, p. 88.
10. *Ibid.*, p. 90.
11. *Ibid.*, p. 99.
12. *Ibid.*, p. 103.
13. 'The Eltham Ordinances, cap. 66', in *Ordinances for the Royal Household*, p. 157.
14. Starkey, *English Court*, p. 165.
15. Quoted from *ibid.*, p. 161.
16. 'The Eltham Ordinances, cap. 61', in *Ordinances for the Royal Household*, p. 156.
17. 'Articles Ordained by King Henry VII for the Regulation of his Household', in *Ordinances for the Royal Household*, p. 116.
18. Sir Robert Naunton, *Fragmenta Regalia*, ed. Edward Arber (1895), p. 17, quoted in Starkey, *English Court*, p. 159.
19. 'The Eltham Ordinances, cap. 70', in *Ordinances for the Royal Household*, p. 158.
20. *Ibid.*, cap. 33, p. 147.
21. Loades, *Tudor Court*, p. 88.
22. Orchard Barker, *Chronicle of the Kings of England* (London, 1643), p. 118.
23. Starkey, *English Court*, p. 152.
24. *Ibid.*, p. 151.
25. Anne Somerset, *Ladies in Waiting from the Tudors to the Present Day* (Weidenfeld & Nicolson, 1984), p. 12.
26. Starkey, *English Court*, p. 148.
27. *Ibid.*, p. 162.
28. 'The Eltham Ordinances, cap. 73', in *Ordinances for the Royal Household*, p. 158.
29. Paul Hentzner, *A Journey into England*, trans. Horace Walpole (London, 1757), pp. 52–3.
30. Somerset, *Ladies in Waiting*, p. 62.
31. *Ibid.*, p. 12.
32. St Clare Byrne (ed.), *The Lisle Letters*, vol. 4, letter 887.
33. Somerset, *Ladies in Waiting*, p. 62.
34. St Clare Byrne (ed.), *The Lisle Letters*, vol. 4, letter 887.
35. Anne Buck, 'The Clothes of Thomasine Petre 1555–1559', *Costume Society Journal*, 24 (1990), 18.
36. St Clare Byrne (ed.), *The Lisle Letters*, vol. 4, p. 194.
37. *Ibid.*, p. 192.
38. *Ibid.*, p. 895.

39. *Ibid.*
40. Loades, *Tudor Court*, p. 48.
41. Thurley, *Royal Palaces*, pp. 130–1.
42. Somerset, *Ladies in Waiting*, p. 62.
43. St Clare Byrne (ed.), *The Lisle Letters*, vol. 4, p. 193.
44. William J. Thomas (ed.), *Anecdotes and Traditions Illustrative of Early English History and Literature* (Camden Society, 1839).
45. Starkey, *English Court*, p. 154.
46. Cavendish, *Life and Death of Cardinal Wolsey*, p. 96.
47. Thurley, *Royal Palaces*, p. 131.
48. 'The Eltham Ordinances, cap. 33', in *Ordinances for the Royal Household*, p. 147.
49. William Jerdan (ed.), *The Rutland Papers. Original Documents Illustrative of the Courts and Times of Henry VII and Henry VIII* (Camden Society, 1842).
50. Alison Sim, 'The Royal Court and Progresses', *History Today* 53 (5) (May 2003), 49.
51. Loades, *Tudor Court*, p. 50.
52. Somerset, *Ladies in Waiting*, p. 62.
53. Henry Clifford, *The Life of the Duchess of Feria* (Burns & Oates, 1887).
54. Somerset, *Elizabeth I*, p. 347.
55. For more information on Tudor marriage, see Sim, *Tudor Housewife*, chapter 1.
56. Somerset, *Ladies in Waiting*, p. 82.
57. Somerset, *Elizabeth I*, p. 348.
58. *Ibid.*, p. 90.
59. Somerset, *Ladies in Waiting*, p. 83.
60. *Ibid.*, p. 14.
61. Arnold, *Queen Elizabeth's Wardrobe Unlock'd*, p. 99.
62. *Ibid.*, p. 103.
63. *Ibid.*, p. 99.
64. *Ibid.*, p. 71.
65. A. Jeffries Collins, *Jewels and Plate of Queen Elizabeth I. The Inventory of 1574*, ed. from Harley MS 1650 and Stowe MS 555 in the British Museum (Trustees of the British Museum, London, 1955), p. 104.
66. Starkey, *English Court*, pp. 162–3.
67. *Ibid.*, p. 157.
68. St Clare Byrne (ed.), *The Lisle Letters*, vol. 4, p. 906.
69. *Ibid.*, p. 887.
70. Clifford, *Life of the Duchess of Feria*, p. 73.

71. 'The Eltham Ordinances, cap. 47', in *Ordinances for the Royal Household*, p. 151.
72. *Ibid.*
73. *Ibid.*, p. 152.
74. *Ibid.*, cap. 48, p. 152.
75. *Ibid.*, cap. 56, p. 155.
76. *Ibid.*, cap. 57, p. 155.
77. *Ibid.*, caps 59, 60 and 67, pp. 156 and 157.
78. *Ibid.*, cap. 45, p. 151.
79. *Ibid.*, cap. 50, pp. 152–3.
80. *Ibid.*, cap. 52, p. 153.
81. J.J. Scarisbrick, *Henry VIII* (Methuen, 1976), p. 638.
82. Hentzner, *Journey into England*, pp. 47–51.
83. 'Articles Ordained by King Henry VII for the Regulation of his Household', p. 121.

Select Bibliography

Below are some of the more modern sources used for this book. The period sources can be traced through the footnotes.

APPRENTICES

Dunlop, O. Jocelyn, *English Apprenticeship and Child Labour* (T. Fisher Unwin, 1912)
Thrupp, Sylvia L., *The Merchant Class of Medieval London* (University of Michigan Press, 1977)
Unwin, George, *The Guilds and Companies of London* (Methuen & Co., 1908)

BLACK SERVANTS

Fryer, Peter, *Staying Power. The History of Black People in Britain* (Pluto Press, 1984)
Jones, Eldred D., *The Elizabethan Image of Africa* (University Press of Virginia for Folger Shakespeare Library, 1971)
Shyllon, F.O., *Black Slaves in Britain* (Oxford University Press for the Institute of Race Relations, 1974)

SERVANTS IN HUSBANDRY

Kussmaul, Ann, *Servants in Husbandry in Early Modern England* (Cambridge University Press, 1981)
Thirsk, Joan (ed.), *The Agrarian History of England and Wales* (Cambridge University Press, 1990)

LIFE IN THE GREAT HOUSEHOLD

Barnett, Richard C., *Place, Profit and Power: A Study of the Servants of William Cecil*, James Sprunt Studies in History and Political Science (University of North Carolina Press, 1969)
Brears, Peter, *All the King's Cooks* (Souvenir Press, 1999)
Charlton, Kenneth, *Education in Renaissance England* (Routledge & Kegan Paul, 1965)
Emmison, F.G., *Tudor Secretary: Sir William Petre at Court and Home* (Longmans, 1961)
Heal, Felicity, *Hospitality in Early Modern England* (Clarendon Press, 1990)
Mertes, Kate, *The English Noble Household 1250–1600* (Basil Blackwell, 1988)
Orme, Nicholas, *From Childhood to Chivalry* (Methuen, 1984)
Stone, Lawrence, *The Crisis of the Aristocracy, 1558–1641* (Clarendon Press, 1965)
——, *Family and Fortune* (Clarendon Press, 1973)
Woodward, Jennifer, *The Theatre of Death* (Boydell Press, 1997)
Woolgar, C.M., *The Great Household in Late Medieval England* (Yale University Press, 1999)

PERSONAL SERVICE TO ROYALTY

Loades, David, *The Tudor Court* (Headstart History, 1992)
Somerset, Anne, *Ladies in Waiting from the Tudors to the Present Day* (Weidenfeld & Nicolson, 1984)
Starkey, David, *The English Court* (Longman, 1987)
Thurley, Simon, *The Royal Palaces of Tudor England* (Yale University Press, 1993)

Index

Index

Index